"Transformational..."
Grace Reynolds

"Best book ever... not even fi___ ___ __ and it has changed my l___
Krystal Smith

"The answers to every question I've ever asked myself and more has already been thought of and answered in this book..."
Karyn Owen

"The most important book I have ever read."
Jesse Dawson

"My Ultimate You journey has enabled me to embrace the real me and fall back in love with who I am in all my perfect imperfections."
Tanya Davis

"Truly empowering..."
Ross Lewis

"I know in my heart this is different than anything I've ever done..."
Kristan Jones

"I'm finally coming out of my shadow and walking tall and actually being myself for the first time in over 60 years... Bring it on!"
Steve Riley

"Life-changing on all levels..."
Mariana Ardelean

"The greatest gift I have ever given me..."
Kylie Hancox

"For the first time in my life I feel like I can breathe, I can truly feel. With the help of Ultimate You, I know exactly where to focus to build the 'Me' I was always meant to be…"

An Sneyers

"My coaching, my marriage and most of all my parenting have taken on a whole new direction. I learned to say 'no' to others, and 'yes' to myself. Meeting my internal needs has given me the foundations to go out into the world and express my ultimate self."

Amy Taylor, Author of *(In)sanity*

"It's a very special feeling to find something incredibly precious that has been lost for a long time. This is how reading and working through Ultimate You feels for me… I had lost ME, and there is now such hope and joy in the promise of a life fully lived, no hiding."

Lyn Carman

"What I am loving about Ultimate You is that I am reconnecting to me. By working on me… I am experiencing much more success in getting the personal and professional results I want. I'd love to say to someone who's thinking of starting this journey that you will create the life you want by working on you. Say yes to Ultimate You."

Jenni Albrecht

"An exceptional body of work that truly helps light the way to becoming our ultimate self and making a deeper difference in the lives of those around us."

John Grant Harvey

"Since starting this journey through taking action, I'm slowly gaining confidence. Today, for first time ever in over 11 years at my job, I got up in front of over 40 people and gave a speech. It's through this Ultimate You journey that I was proud to stand by what I believe in and spread this message publicly. It starts with me…"

Candice Protheroe

"I have moved from a people-pleaser to living each day with absolute clarity around what is important to me. I have reclaimed me and I am free and empowered to live in ways I would never have dared to dream before. If you are living day to day in a life that does not rock your world, I recommend doing yourself a favor and read your way through this incredible life-changing book…"

Liz Murray

"I am thrilled to be rediscovering my true self. Today my life is not run by other people's needs, wants and values. Because I have new thinking models and language, I am redefining success on my terms in business and in life."

Lia Zalums

"As Sharon taught the models in this book and spoke of feelings I thought only belonged to me, I realized there was nothing wrong with me, I had simply misplaced me. And so began the amazing journey… Only 13 months after that transformational day, I was full-time in my own business as a writer and creative success strategist. I found my purpose in my I-amness…"

Karen McTackett, Author of *The Human Concept*

"I have read many brilliant books on personal development yet Ultimate You has taken me on the deepest dive into my inner world. It has guided me on a step by step journey towards becoming my ultimate self. Totally inspiring…"

Jane Cann

"As you hold this book in your hands, you are about to step into a place of unknown, excitement, love and so much more. You're about to embark on a beautiful adventure that will make a huge difference in your life if you choose for it to. So take the pages that follow as a gift, for life. A gift that will keep giving, that you will want to revisit more than once…"

Nicky Miklos-Woodley

"Ultimate You has to be by far the best book I have ever read. To get the mind thinking of why I am the way I am… and the choices I make. I want to be the best version of me. No stone left unturned. Thank you!"

Deb Pace

"I love that you have a strategy, not fluff. This is easy to understand and explore. It's not a quick fix but a journey worth exploring and living."

Phillip Evans

"I've learnt to ground myself from the inside out…
I've learnt to meet my own needs in resourceful ways…
I've learnt to back myself and champion myself…
I've learnt to ask for what I need…
I've learnt to embrace all of me, warts and all…
I've learnt not to suppress my feeling but rather move through
them with awareness, understanding and compassion…
I've learnt I can be an awesome leader for my family, loved ones
and for those who resonate with my message…
I've learnt so many structures to support my dream and connect with
my soul, so I can live my life to my fullest and in alignment
with my highest values and beliefs…
So much learning and this is only the tip of the iceberg!"

Sonya Maree Kok

"Giving myself control over my own life is the best thing I've learned from this… I am finally beginning to understand the words 'you already have everything you need within you.' This should be in schools."

Misty Forsman

"Ultimate You helped me understand why I am the way I am. It is challenging and confronting… But it gives you an incredible hope that this is going to be OK."

Stephen O'Keefe

Other Books by Sharon Pearson

Ultimate You Quest Edition

Disruptive Leadership

Simple Strategies for Business Success

Your Success

Dedication

This book is dedicated to

_____

* This book is dedicated to you.
Go ahead and put your name in the space.

ULTIMATE

Heal. Reclaim. Become.

YOU

Live Your Awesome Life.

SHARON PEARSON

International Bestselling Author

Waterside Productions

GLOBAL SUCCESS
INSTITUTE

ULTIMATE YOU

Pearson, Sharon

First published 2019

Phone: (+61) 3 9645 9945

Email: support@globalsuccessinstitute.com

Website: www.globalsuccessinstitute.com

Published by Waterside Productions

2055 Oxford Avenue, Cardiff, CA 92007

The Global Success Institute,
Suite 40, 37-39 Albert Road, Melbourne,
VIC 3004, Australia.

ISBN-13: 978-1-941768-08-2 print edition
ISBN-13: 978-1-941768-11-2 ebook edition
ISBN-13: 978-1-941768-12-9 audio edition

For accompanying book resources and supporting materials, please visit
www.ultimateyouquest.com/quest-support

Table of Contents

Foreword

Many years ago I was on a speaking tour in Australia and had the chance to meet Sharon. This was the beginning of our wonderful friendship. Not only was she a sponge for getting to know me quickly at a deep level, she was also willing to be extremely vulnerable in revealing to me the trials and tribulations of her own life.

What impressed me specifically was how she shared the lowest and highest points of her epic journey – from being suicidal to mastering her thoughts and her emotions in order to become centered and focused and all that she's meant to be. I recall her relaying how she was tired of being a victim of depression and of her circumstances and how she had finally decided to break free and be victorious by taking control of her life.

To say she succeeded would be an understatement, for today she owns a mega-successful coaching school dedicated to helping others recognize and release whatever is holding them back from achieving their goals and dreams. In essence, she took her life's mess and turned it into her message, and positively impacting the world with her powerful and transformative insights and her kind heart.

Over the years I've observed and loved several of her amazing character traits, which you will find detailed in this book. She plays life full-out and gives without reservation. In this, she is one of the most generous and positive human beings I have ever met. In addition, she has a mindset that consistently manifests abundance.

Sharon is also a voracious student committed to consistently upgrading her knowledge and skills in order to improve on them and share the benefits of what she has learned with others. As a result, she's one of the most impactful teachers and coaches in the world, emphasizing that it's not your circumstances that shape your destiny, rather your choices and decisions do.

In reading this book you will enjoy the simplicity with which she reveals how you too can restore your centeredness and wholeness… what Sharon calls your "Centered Self".

What will also become apparent is that achieving the life you want and were destined to have is an inside-out game – and once you take that first important step of nurturing, cherishing, and trusting your Inner World, you begin to claim your own unique self.

There's an inscription over the ancient Greek temple at Delphi that reads "Know Thyself."

What does it really mean to know thyself?

It means not being afraid to look deep inside to evaluate your beliefs, stories, excuses, strengths, skills, weaknesses, failures, and successes.

If you're ready to enter a journey of self-awareness and discovery that will transform your life, make sure you fully absorb the words on each page of this book and consciously apply their wisdom to your life. In doing so you will give yourself the life-changing gift of knowing your truest self, free of fear and self-doubt.

The most important relationship you can ever have is with the person in the mirror, and being truthful and honest with yourself is your ticket to freedom and having the life you've always dreamed of.

Choose to let go of what hasn't worked in the past and, starting today, choose to master your inner game so that your life becomes the very special masterpiece it was meant to be.

John Assaraf

*John Assaraf is one of the leading mindset and behavior experts in the world. He is the author of two New York Times bestselling books, **Having It All** and **The Answer**. He is also the author of **Innercise: The New Science to Unlock Your Brain's Hidden Power**. He has appeared numerous times on Larry King Live, Anderson Cooper, and The Ellen DeGeneres Show. Today, he is the Founder and CEO of NeuroGym, a company dedicated to using the most advanced technologies and evidence-based brain-training methods to help individuals unleash their fullest potential.*

Introduction

Unveiling the Masterpiece Inside

"What lies behind us and what lies before us are tiny matters compared to what lies within us."

Attributed to Ralph Waldo Emerson

I'm going to take a leap here and say you're reading these lines because you're searching for answers to questions that are out of focus, but you know are essential. You know that "something" has to change, and you have a sneaking suspicion that something is you.

You have no idea what to do with these questions, but what you *do* know is that you're tired of hearing that the answers are within. You've looked. The answers weren't there. I remember I got to feel extra-bad about myself when I looked within and found insecurity, unworthiness, and fear.

In some ways, it's easier just to look away. To close this book and pretend that your feelings of inner disquiet will fade, or that they don't matter all that much, or "that's just how it is."

But then you have the disturbing sense that you're missing out on living life fully. You sense the uncomfortable truth within you: that self-esteem, self-love, and self-worth just shouldn't be this difficult to embrace and claim as your own. You have the growing realization that joy, fearlessness, and active compassion should be attributes of your natural state.

So here we are. You… facing the possibility that you may be holding "the answers," but perhaps skeptical that they even exist. Me… holding the space as I extend my invitation to you to take that leap one more time with the hope that's within you right now – so that together we can uncover the hidden truth of you. And just perhaps, set you off on the adventure of your life.

I remember thinking: *If life is supposed to be this grand adventure, where's mine?* I was struggling on the outside and struggling even more on the inside. I was depressed and suicidal and, as my suicidal thoughts grew, it occurred to me that I must have trained my mind to hit the auto-destruct button by mistake.

I've learned there are two ways we can live our lives.

One is where we're on "automatic". In this mode we passively react to what happens to us, abdicating responsibility as to how matters unfold, playing defense in the hopes that the worst life has to offer will somehow pass us by.

The other is what's called "conscious living". This is us in full bad-ass mode, embracing our life with joy, fearlessness, and compassion, unselfconsciously being our True Self and loving all of it.

Which path we take is the difference between merely surviving and totally thriving.

I call conscious living "Your Awesome Life". Taste the wonder of embracing life, fully present to the moment; with freedom from the shame of not being enough; with a dancing heart and the intention to know your own precious truth.

To get you back on the path to Your Awesome Life, you're going to restore the You that you were meant to be. You know who I mean… the You who is compassionate, loving, warm, open, adventurous, resilient, and adaptable, and feels they're worthy, and utterly – without condition – lovable. This version of you – your Centered Self – has more than likely gone into hiding, having been suppressed, denied, rejected, shut down, judged, ignored, and shamed.

This is largely the work of your Guardian – another obstacle on the path to Your Awesome Life. The Guardian is the mask you wear because this is who you think you "should" be. Your Guardian was trained in your childhood to defend you. This training was informed by your family and other significant people in your life. They might be your parents, foster parents, siblings, a teacher, or a priest, for example. We'll call them your "Big People".

This Guardian has tried to keep you safe from hurt, protect you from feeling abandoned, and done all it can to guard you against ever feeling ashamed. Unfortunately, your Guardian is also the source of your low self-esteem; why you think you're "fake" or why you feel so misunderstood. When we meet this protector of yours, we will have traveled a journey to reclaim and restore the full truth of you, and you'll be ready to let your Guardian take a break as your Centered Self steps forward to replace it.

So I'm going to invite you, when you're ready, to question how you've learned to defend yourself, and perhaps discover, as Neo did when learning about the Matrix in the movie of the same name, that *there is another path*.

As with every great story, you are the hero of this tale – the conductor of your own symphony. It may seem that the world "Out There" is determining your fate and your feelings, but please know that your path will lead you to the one constant truth: the answers you seek *are* within you. Trust that although today, in this very moment, you may not know *precisely* how or where to look within, you *will* learn, and you will see the truth of how empowered you can be.

In Part I of this book – "I Can… Heal" – you get to lay the foundation stones for Your Awesome Life by reclaiming your most precious and valuable gift: your own mind. You want it to work for you, not against you!

Part II – "I Will Reclaim" – is the more profound work where you restore the three essential elements of your self-esteem. It's a wonderful, challenging, and ultimately life-affirming journey to your Centered Self – the core of you – where you embody compassion, joy, and utter fearlessness.

Part III – "I Become" – is where you learn how to let go of the need for drama, fear, overthinking, and procrastination, and replace it with the truth that you are enough, you are worthy, and you are lovable. Here you dive into conscious living and make life- and love-affirming choices that align with your Centered Self and help you on the path to Your Awesome Life. And in every chapter, there are plenty of other ideas about how best to embrace Your Awesome Life, as well as more examples, stories, and guidance.

This journey, for me, is a lifelong one. The information contained in this book details how I'm consistently guiding myself to restore my Truest Self, and how I'm guiding thousands of other people as they navigate in the direction of their own Awesome Lives.

To be authentic, and to have your life filled with the delicious joy of you, this journey can't be done in your head. You can't think your way to your Awesome Life. It's a journey that can only be known through the steps *you* take. As Morpheus shares with Neo, there is a difference between knowing the path and walking the path.

To help welcome you to your transformation, a video from me to you, as well as some other resources, can be found here:

www.ultimateyouquest.com/quest-support

I invite you to visit these resources – for they are foundational to your process of transformation.

Within you is a fire that burns brightly – without apology and without self-consciousness. Your Centered Self is open to life and to love and awaits…

RESOURCES FOR YOUR JOURNEY

A companion worksheet, an exercise for you to do that relates to this section, a video from me, and more resources are available for you at:

www.ultimateyouquest.com/quest-support

PART I

"I Can... Heal"

Part I of this quest you and I are on is about laying the groundwork as we begin to build your vision of yourself. It's the stuff that's out of sight, but vital. You wouldn't build a house on soft sand, and nor should you seek Your Awesome Life without some sense of how to go about that.

I remember being frustrated by so many self-help, goal-setting books that talked about fear but didn't talk about what to do with the source of that fear. Or they told me to "Just do it!" when I had no clue what that meant. Or the message was for me to live my dream when I felt this was somehow impossible but couldn't pinpoint why.

It's so simple to say "Overcome your fear," or "Live your dream." It's much less simple to free yourself of the invisible quicksand that holds you back. But after working with so many people who share the same frustration and the same sense of failure because "Just do it!" didn't work for them, we're going to approach this differently.

In this first part of this quest, let's do our best to *wake up*.

We both know the feeling of living in a waking trance where we see ourselves react in ways we've always reacted, feel disappointed in ourselves, and have drifted further and further from the belief that our life has meaning.

And we've both experienced trying to move forward with our lives and then feeling overwhelmed by intangible forces pulling us back to a status quo we desperately want to leave behind.

And hopefully you're also in touch with the moments in your life where you feel connection to a deeper truth within you; the inescapable, glorious knowing that you matter, you're lovable, and you're enough.

To have more moments of this truth, we're going to visit three aspects of ourselves that are always present, even when we deny them. We're going to accept the gift of *empowerment*, and discover where we feel most gathered and grounded. We're going to ignite within ourselves the capacity to live *consciously*, so we can tune in to what resonates with us beyond the clutter and noise of our fears. And we're going to claim the gift of freedom from our past conditioning, and so embrace attaching ourselves to something magnificent – our own sense of who we are.

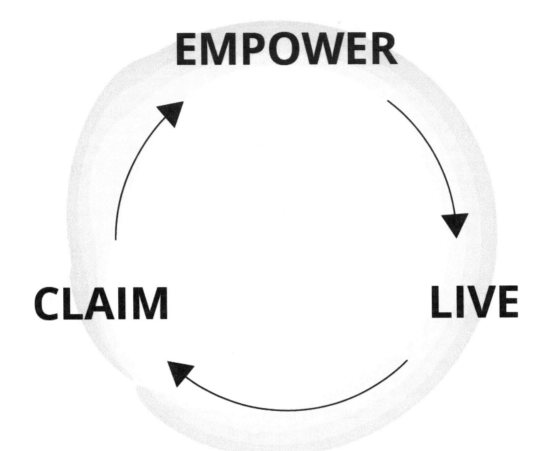

RESOURCES FOR YOUR JOURNEY

A companion worksheet, an exercise for you to do that relates to this section, a video from me, and more resources are available for you at:

www.ultimateyouquest.com/quest-support

CHAPTER 1

Your First Gift:
Your Empowered Mind

"Wherever you are, be there totally.
If you find your here and now intolerable and it makes you
unhappy, you have three options: remove yourself from the
situation, change it, or accept it totally.
If you want to take responsibility for your life,
you must choose one of those three options,
and you must choose now.
Then accept the consequences."

Eckhart Tolle

Just consider for a moment the possibility that you have within you an infinite reservoir of resourcefulness, compassion, resilience, and courage. What if, despite the negative press you give yourself, you were born naturally adventurous, lovable, worthy, brave, and curious about your world? Perhaps your view of these possibilities is being blocked by some limiting beliefs, habits, and choices that, instead of celebrating the awesome you, encourage you to hide, avoid life, and delay your dreams.

Then imagine you're with a young child who is filled with all of these wonderful possibilities. She is adventurous, open, and curious about her world and unable to comprehend that you're not this way too.

Now imagine that for some crazy reason you're going to try to convince this young, precious child that your view is right, and she should feel the same as you do.

What would you say to her? What tone would you use? How would your demeanor be? How might she react? If she was upset by what you said, how would you feel about that?

It would be a mad, sick joke to ever do this to a child…

Yet isn't that what you do to yourself, each and every day?

If you and I are going to take this journey together, how about we commit, right now, to embrace the idea that perhaps… just perhaps… the possibilities we see so easily in a child we can restore and celebrate within ourselves.

I invite you to entertain the thought that, as you've grown up, you've allowed your spirit to be dampened and the You that you are to go into hiding.

I would also invite you to acknowledge that things don't have to be this way. They shouldn't be this way! You should just be madly, completely, head over heels in love with who you are and who you're becoming, with no apology and no shame. Just laugh-out-f*cking-loud delighted with yourself as you embrace your fearlessness, your joy, and your compassion for yourself, for the people in your life, and for this very moment.

You are the universe you're experiencing, and the magic you seek... is you!

It amazes me how many people think they're going to arrive at this happy place through wishful thinking, avoiding challenges, living in their comfort zone, letting time go by, or through "trusting things will get better." They react to life, seem mystified by their lack of progress, and then blame someone or something or their past, as if this will magically rectify the injustice of their situation.

The truth is that no amount of magic – or wishful thinking – can ever auto-correct the feeling of staggering under the weight of a life less than fully lived.

You and I are not the exceptions here. The universe isn't operating somehow separately for either of us. The truth is that "It" is not operating at all…

You are.

You Are a Product of Your Past Conditioning

How you got where you are at this precise moment in your life is a function of biology, psychology, your past, the culture in which you were raised, the way you were perceived as a child, the media you consume, the way you spend your day – as well as endless other factors that range from the incredibly significant to the barely noticeable. And you got here just as much based on the experiences you *didn't* have – the fact that you may not have been raised as a princess in England means you don't have access to that world and the expectations that come along with it.

So in terms of where you are right now, what you *didn't experience* is as significant as what you *did* experience and have come to accept as truth.

So the question then becomes: **are you aware of the experiences, truths, ideas, beliefs, perceptions, and choices that will empower you and help you live Your Awesome Life?**

This question becomes incredibly pressing if your life is less than delightful, if you feel you're somehow unworthy or unlovable, or if you want to take life in your arms and embrace it. It becomes *the* most pressing question if you want to do something about it.

First, let's explore what the building blocks to Your Awesome Life consist of. And let's agree that no matter how much we don't want it to be so, *each of us is entirely in charge of what we're willing to learn, to change, to do, and to let go of on our journey to what I call our "Centered Self"*.

> "If you want to create the life of your dreams, then you are going to have to take 100% responsibility for your life... That means giving up all your excuses, all your victim stories, all the reasons why you can't and why you haven't up until now, and all your blaming of outside circumstances. You have to give them all up forever."

Jack Canfield, The Success Principles

This is your first gift – your phenomenal, empowered mind.

It's working as you've instructed it to work. It's operating based on your beliefs and your expectations and your directions – it couldn't do anything else!

Now you're going to empower it with what it needs so you can begin your journey to your Centered Self. **Your Centered Self is the very core of you; it's where you feel compassion, fearlessness, and joy. It's the Truest You, where you complete yourself, know you're enough, know you're lovable and know you're worthy.** All of us have a Centered Self, and yet many if not most of us aren't in touch with it. This is because we've buried it beneath loads of wishful thinking and assumptions and the desire for things to change of their own accord.

What Does Being Empowered Really Mean?

This is what *empowered* means to me... It's when you know that how you respond to life is how you respond to yourself. So there are two questions for us both to consider.

1. Is being empowered going to help you live Your Awesome Life?
2. If so, what are the building blocks of this empowerment?

I'd like to suggest to you that when you know life is simply a reflection of your own perceptions, beliefs, attitudes, expectations, and choices then being empowered becomes vitally important. Especially if you don't *feel* empowered! To explore this a little further, I invite you to challenge whatever "truths" you've been holding onto and question them. If they don't meet the standard of helping you to feel and be empowered, then they have a lot to answer for. Ask yourself, "Am I allowing my most empowered self to chart the course of my life?"

Now consider the following empowerment "truths" and trust that they're true for you, regardless of what's happening in your life right now.

- *You are responsible for your life*, your choices, your responses, your thoughts, and your feelings. You love this and welcome the adventure of discovery as you reveal more of who you are by identifying what you take responsibility for.
- *You don't lie to yourself.* You are committed to you. You give yourself honest appraisal about how you're doing and where you need to lift your game. You say what you mean and mean what you say without equivocation or resentment. There is joy in commitment because it brings you closer to your Centered Self. You don't hide behind platitudes or distractions to kid yourself that it's all good.
- Rather than wishing, waiting, and hoping for "things" to change or improve, *you are the catalyst for the change you want to see in your life.*
- There's no pause in your life as you wait to figure out what's wrong with you or wish to feel more confident. *You're living life fully* as you figure yourself out.
- *You make mistakes, learn, improve, and move on,* rather than fearing mistakes and only doing what you believe you can get "right". There's genuine freedom within you as you welcome challenges, which are really moments to grow.
- *No one has to change for you to live your life*, for you are free of the need to control or manipulate others or to be controlled or manipulated by them. *No one has to rescue you.*

In accepting all of these empowerment truths, you're getting behind the wall of defenses of your mind. Behind that wall, you may find the old constructs of wishful thinking about how life is supposed to unfold, perceived injustices you may be holding onto, and assumptions you've been making about how "you" don't have to change for "things" to change. Once you get past all of these old beliefs, you've taken the first step to banish them.

How you got to where you are is far less significant than what you do about it

Only You Can Rescue You

You were a child, and through no fault of your own, your Centered Self – your Truest Self – went into hiding – and she's stayed there ever since. She needs you; oh, my goodness how she needs you, to be fierce and determined and "grrrr" about her restoration.

Perhaps you've been lulled into thinking it's "normal" to be placid about your life and oh so "stoic" as things go to shit. Or perhaps you've come to accept that being angry at all the injustices is somehow the way to live. Maybe you believe that if you play the victim in your relationships, you'll finally be saved.

You may have yourself on the hamster wheel of thinking that being righteous, and proving others wrong is how you should be.

Perhaps procrastination is normal to you.

You may accept it as natural to please others and have yourself last on your to-do list.

Perhaps you've created a lot of drama around being wounded, being misunderstood, being more religious, being smarter, or being perfect, and you relentlessly defend this stance.

Perhaps your flavor of "normal" is to be heroic and super-helpful and all-capable and sadness-free.

Or maybe you've never questioned how you don't seem to feel strong emotions, no matter what's going on, and think it's kinda weird (or even kinda weak) that others do.

Or you've set things up in such a way that everyone takes you for granted.

Or you're measured by how much you give.

Or you're seen as the "black sheep" of the family.

There are so many versions of "this is how I'm supposed to be," and these are only a few.

Again, is any of this moving you toward your empowered self? Your Awesome Life? Your Centered and Truest Self? Of course not.

So it's time to hit the pause button and recognize, whatever… *whatever*… your pattern of business-as-usual is, it's time to question it, reassess it, and just possibly dump it as the saboteur it is.

As Dr. David Burns shares in his book, *Ten Days to Self-Esteem*, "I have discovered that one of the most important keys to recovery, regardless of your age, sex, or race, is the willingness to help yourself."

You Are Responsible

Your empowerment won't come about by wishfully imagining that some set of circumstances will vanish, or someone else will miraculously see things your way, or because a prayer for things to get easier is answered.

You are the answer to all your prayers,
to all your problems, and to all the misfortune
you may have or be still experiencing

I was my own, first, terrible client. I wanted no part of this philosophy of self-reliance when I first heard it. I'd convinced myself that blaming my parents, my illnesses, my bad luck, and my insecurities were my only option in life. And I was masterful at it.

I was also sick and tired, depressed, isolated, and righteous. I was miserable, and if you were around me at that time, thanks for not sharing with me how miserable I no doubt made you.

Just consider what or who you blame, or what excuses you make, or how you justify what's going on in any area of your life – your health, your money, your relationships, your career, your home, your education – and then look more closely at that specific area. I'm going to guess, with a reasonable degree of accuracy, that you will find some pretty well-defended rationalizations for why things are the way they are.

For the longest time, I told myself that the reason I wasn't wealthy was because I'd been raised to believe struggling financially was how it was supposed to be.

When I challenged my own BS, I saw how I was sitting safely in the cheap seats criticizing people who were Out There hustling. I was willfully trashing years of my own life on blame and excuses, and when I realized this, I quit complaining and blaming and justifying and instead decided to at least *try* to be responsible for my life. I wondered, *What if, after years of desperation, I had this power all along? What if it was in me from the get-go?*

Turns out, it was.

I became wealthy only when I changed where I placed my responsibility for my results. I felt more empowered because I owned my BS, challenged it, and found another way. As I became more empowered, I was able to let go of the idea that I had to struggle financially.

More recently, I've been learning to shift responsibility for my relationships from "people are so selfish" to how *I'm* showing up. Have you ever noticed how it's easier to blame "them", rather than see the gaps in ourselves? Or is that just me being petty and ashamed because I knew I'd been hiding and couldn't convince myself any longer that this blame-them-and-duck strategy wasn't going to lead to my own personal empowerment?

This has been a raw journey filled with potholes from my past. I'd spent years convinced that I was a good friend because I put others first and never shared my problems. Sounds lovely, until I realized it was a form of control. As in, all out, keep-em-at-a-distance-don't-let-anyone-get-too-close warfare strategy where I got to feel superior as long as others told me their issues and I acted as if I was issue-free. I know, it's so obvious now, right? Yet Back Then I could say with my hand on my heart that I was a good person.

So why did I feel so alone?

Responsibility is the joy of knowing that
you can find a way

I know you know this and it's just a gentle reminder… when you are your Truest Self you're not the victim. You may have earned a few scars that life has handed out, but you're not defeated and you don't quit. You heal. You replenish. You figure out where you can adapt for next time so that you emerge, wiser, more resolute and more tuned into what works for you. You don't sit in dismay and you don't plot revenge. You don't sulk, rage, or shut down. You rally. You get the hell back up. And you own it.

You've got this. No matter the challenge, you get what you can handle. Nothing more, nothing less.

Whatever isn't working for you in your life, assume, regardless of whether it's true or not, that it's up to you. That it *is* you. No matter how it presses every button in you. No matter how much emotional reactivity you have to it. No matter how much you believe you can have one hand pointing at someone and one hand on the Bible and say "It's them."

Because as long as you act as if you're powerless, you stay stuck exactly where you are, an autumn leaf, blown where the wind takes you then swept and dumped where the gutter catches you, at the whim of whatever external force impacts you.

Sam Harris, philosopher, neuroscientist, and "thinker in public" shares in his book *Waking Up: A Guide to Spirituality Without Religion*, "My mind begins to seem like a video game: I can either play it intelligently, learning more in each round, or I can be killed in the same spot by the same monster, again and again."

If being empowered doesn't seem so available to you right now, that's okay. Just stretch yourself as far as you can, and we'll do all of this again tomorrow, and the next day. None of this is an all-or-nothing kind of deal. For me and for many others it's been more of a let's-see-what-I'm-noticing-today kind of journey. That's moving us in the direction of Our Awesome Lives, which sure as hell beats the alternative.

No More Lies

Back Then, or what I affectionately call "the Beginning of Me Waking The Hell Up," I liked being in my bubble of denial because I was so addicted to simple, straightforward, black-and-white thinking. Back then the complexity and ambiguity of life was unimaginably scary and unmanageable. Best play it safe. Best stay small. Best keep hidden. Best not stand out. Best not even try.

So I pretended to myself that I would take a massive leap towards getting my life together… *another time.*

This was my great lie.

And I had lots of little lies to keep it company. My self-esteem will improve… *somehow.* My fear will fade… *in a while.* My lack of friends will fix itself… *when people realize I'm right.* My comfort zone may be shrinking, but I know I'll do something to break out of it… *when I believe in myself.* I can't change my life today… *not until I've fixed myself.* It's not that I'm holding myself back… *I'm just constantly misunderstood.* Yes, I feel depressed and sad… *but it's got nothing to do with how badly I treat myself.* I'm miserable… *and it's just how it is.*

And on it went. Endless answers to my own pain, which were all created with one pretty serious design defect… they guaranteed my misery. These weren't lies I told myself so that one day I might actually arrive at My Awesome Life. They were lies that were literally *designed* to give me misery.

I pacified myself into a lull of complacent acceptance until my world consisted of so many lies that I had to defend. Breaking out of my day-to-day misery never occurred to me. To break out would have been to admit the entire house of cards upon which I'd built my internal world was a lie.

I'd walled myself into a tiny space, where even breathing became difficult. Everything outside of this narrow, confined space was overwhelming and beyond me, and reminded me how little I knew about how to really, truly, deeply… live.

So of course the obvious thing to do was to block out the wonderful world Out There. To do this with any measure of success, I had to become, for a short while, shut inside my house, too scared to venture out. This was not just because the world was *big*, but because I'd trained my thinking to become so incredibly small.

I was a prisoner of my own making. I often told myself Back Then that I wasn't successful. Yet when I think about the lengths I went to, the determination I showed, and the tenacity I demonstrated to stay in this prison, I would say I knew how to succeed. I was just succeeding at *really* dumb, self-sabotaging stuff.

My wake-up call happened on a regular day, just like any other – except on this day I found myself frozen with fear. Just the thought of walking to the kitchen to make a cup of tea filled me with terror.

So I remained rooted in one spot in my living room, knowing that whatever direction I took, I would feel like a failure. And it occurred to me that there were plenty of people in the world who'd had awful, heartbreaking upbringings who had gone on to triumph over their pain and lead lives of epic proportion. And although I'd had my fair share of heartbreak, my life until then was... mundane... compared to the depths of their despair before their having risen to become the best version of themselves they could possibly be. I thought about Oprah. Mandela. People who were doing whatever they could to triumph over their very real heartaches.

What. On. Earth. Was. My. Excuse?

Or excuses, I should say. I knew I had a stack of them but I'd never challenged them. I'd just gone along with them, assuming they were right and true.

I was thirty-seven. And I'd invested – dedicated – all those years to a set of beliefs, the sum total impact of which was that I was now rooted to the spot with fear at the thought of walking across my living room.

I'd been lying to myself, and the wake-up call was the ice-cold bucket of water I needed. Admittedly (because I hate to be wrong) I spent two weeks after this realization crying over the wasted years and how I'd deceived myself.

As I stood there in my living room, paralyzed with my own stories, I committed to dedicating my *next* thirty-seven years to figuring out what My Awesome Life looked like, and what it would take to achieve it.

The first thing I did, and I invite you to do the same thing if you relate to any of what I've just shared, is to face your lies – the little ones that seem so harmless, and the bigger ones that you just know are getting in your way of your great mission to live Your Awesome Life.

And then, begin to slowly, gently, and a little fiercely, replace the BS with the big truths. These are the truths that will move you toward your own empowerment. Here are a few big truths that I hold dear today, but which have taken more than a few years to become *my* truths:

1. **What you're willing to do today is what you'll be willing to do tomorrow.** That's the truth. If you're not going to do it today, dump the BS that tomorrow will be different. Instead, do a little something today. Just enough so you live this truth. Your empowerment depends on it.

2. **How you do the little things is how you do everything.** No more hiding. If you treat the little moments like they don't matter, you're going to keep having moments that don't matter. Make them matter. Make this moment, right now, matter. Give this moment your attention, your focus, your appreciation.

3. **Imperfect action beats perfect planning.** Or, to put it a little more directly, doing something is better than doing nothing. Your procrastination – which you justify as "planning," "thinking," "waiting for the right time" – is BS. Do something today that your future self will thank you for. Special note to the perfectionists: For goodness sake, you've tried doing things your way! If it was a sure-fire, champion, winner of an idea, wouldn't the sages have written about it for hundreds of years? Yet everywhere I look, and everyone I listen to who knows how to live fully seems to be getting Out There and taking imperfect action and improving through actual effort. Special, special note to the control freaks: You are not the exception.

4. **You tune into your empowerment when you keep your promises to yourself.** Every promise you keep to yourself is a deposit into your empowerment bank. Each and every time you make a commitment to yourself that you don't keep, your sense of empowerment drops and your Centered Self retreats. Stop, right now, with the "I'm gonna…" and replace it with, "I may…," "I choose…," "I am delaying this, and I'm being honest to myself about it…"

5. **Your Centered Self is hungry for you to only make promises that you will keep.** Every promise you make and keep to another builds your sense of empowerment and empowers your relationships as well.

You Were Born to Have the Life You Deserve, and That's Exactly What You're Getting

Making decisions for yourself about the life you wanted wasn't available to you as a child. It was in the hands of the people who raised you and contributed to your upbringing. They include your family, the people you were in touch with as you grew up, and your school and its teachers. Today… whether you own where you're at or believe it's not up to you, you are getting the life you deserve.

No more lies. Only the truth. And when you forget, as I often did but less so now, give yourself a gentle reminder. Nothing too harsh. Let it contain compassion for yourself. And acknowledgment to yourself that you're making progress.

Whatever your big lie is, and no matter what your little lies have been, it's okay to face them. It's also okay to feel a bit uncomfortable when you do this. In fact, it's normal. Do it anyway, because as we're going to explore later, you, honestly facing yourself and then staying with it, is the key to unlocking your Centered Self.

This is the Sign You've Been Looking For…

Have you noticed how we're often encouraged to look for our meaningful and fulfilled lives by placing trust in forces outside of ourselves, and then we're asked to believe "they" will take care of things? Success. Crystals. Psychics. Sex. The Spirits. The Fates. Karma. Signs. Tarot. Synchronicities. Magic Charms. Astrological signs. Power. Money. The "perfect" partner.

We're encouraged to look for these things anywhere, it would seem, but within ourselves.

And it makes sense why it would be this way. Looking within is uncomfortably hard, sometimes excruciatingly hard. I say this from experience. When something outside of us gives us a "clue" or a sign as to which way to inform our decisions, and it turns out to be wrong, it's so easy to justify it… *Not the right time… I need to become more spiritual… It has a meaning I haven't uncovered yet… Mysterious…* Or easier still, when we *like* the answer we receive, and we act accordingly. In this case, we don't have to think too deeply about it, its repercussions, or whether it's truly aligned with who we are and who we're becoming.

To look outside of yourself for guidance is, don't you think, a lot simpler than to look within yourself, not find an answer, and then admit we don't know what to do about it? For a long time, my looking within felt like a short ride to hell. Too much chaos. Uncertainty. Fear. Reminders of my flaws. Scenes of the mistakes I was yet to make. Or my personal specialty… believing that disaster was imminent all the time.

If you have a particular way of seeking the truth "Out There" and you feel like you need to defend it right now, just read the next few sentences before you skip this section, please.

If you grew up encouraged to look within to find answers for yourself, which allowed and encouraged you to develop your own set of values, beliefs, expectations, and perceptions independent of your tribe, you're an anomaly on the planet. Second, you wouldn't equate "Out There" mystical guidance, or a desire to win, or a hunger to have the… relationship… car… career… as the path for you to transition from confusion to clarity.

Looking to an external sign for guidance wouldn't even be something you would consider turning to, because you would have such a deep sense of self-trust, which you knew you could count on to be relentlessly accurate. You already would have those most precious of elusive gifts… sound judgment, wisdom, patience, compassion, good humor, resilience, calm in the face of the inevitable storms of life and an ability to adjust and bounce back should your decisions miss the mark.

If you've been raised, like most of us, in a way that *did* impose its preferences, beliefs, expectations – even demands – onto you, then turning away from yourself and towards some external impetus for your decisions seems natural.

Because of this, you would struggle to see your Inner World as a source of guidance, comfort, wisdom, calm or certainty. You feel undernourished when you look within.

If you've been raised as most people have, I'd go even further and say that rather than being a source of comfort and love, your Inner World is *the source* of much of your pain and confusion.

And this becomes a self-fulfilling loop. You don't have a developed Inner World to draw on with repetitive reliability, so you go outside of yourself for answers, which means your Inner World falls into greater disrepair, which makes it even harder to turn within for much needed guidance. So you go outside yourself for this, and the loop of all that discontent continues and frequently accelerates.

We all need a level of certainty in the midst of the chaos of life. If we can't detect trust within ourselves, then suspicion, superstition, and self-doubt creeps in. We either feel we can handle the stuff of life, or we fill the gap of doubt with superstition and suspicion. And the bigger the gap, the more "signs" and indicators from outside of us we come to depend on.

*The closer you move toward restoring your
Centered Self, the more grounded, resilient, capable,
and awe-inspiring you feel about yourself*

It's inevitable that when you want something, there will be obstacles to overcome. If there were no obstacles, you would achieve the goal just by wishing it was achieved. That's what's significant about achieving a goal. It's not whether or not you "won". It's whether or not you're a better person for the experience. It's whether you learned from what happened… Whether you trusted yourself. Whether you handled what happened with calm resilience. Whether you discovered an aspect of you which is wonderful. You find out who you truly are when the pressure is on and the convenient thing to do would be to quit.

But if you see obstacles as a "sign" you shouldn't do something, you won't give this hard stuff a go, and you won't become the person you admire. You're drawing on your Outer World for "clues" about what the "universe" is telling you, instead of finding out who you really are.

*Obstacles are a sign you're doing something
you care about and that matters to you:
It's a great sign that you have discovered what
you need to learn to achieve your goal*

News Flash: Your Flaws Aren't That Fascinating

You and I have what I call a "Guardian". It's the mask we wear in public so that people don't see the "real" us. We don't believe we can reveal our true selves, or we've been discouraged from doing so, or we don't like what we see, so we stay hidden. This false self – the part of you that currently runs the show, thinks it has all the answers, tries to keep you safe, seeks to protect you from ever feeling vulnerable yet strong, denies you compassion and doesn't think there's anything wrong with you feeling self-doubt – is right now resisting the messages of this book. They're scary to your Guardian because they challenge its very existence. If you're authentically, fully, and unselfconsciously living your own conscious life, your Guardian's purpose has ended.

More than anything else, your Guardian wants you to be safe. Never mind that the definition of this safety is for you to play a small game, stay in your lane, not be vulnerable, and not love yourself. To help you get hooked and addicted to safety, it plays a head game with you. This head game is called "let's undermine your every move."

You know the one. You're thinking… just *thinking* for goodness sake… of trying something new. And what's the very next thing you're thinking about? You're now listening to your mind try to talk you out of it, as it helpfully reminds you of all your flaws and all the ways you've failed in the past. *Thanks, brain.*

Instead of trying the new adventure, you're now plunged into self-doubt and listing your flaws; all the while your Guardian is thinking: *crisis averted.*

So let's just stop the record for a moment and think this through. This whole chapter is about your empowerment. Has reminding yourself of your flaws ever helped you feel empowered?

Ever?

Could it?

At your core, you know the truth. Life is happening right now. Ready or not. And no amount of self-reflection without action is going to make you feel empowered, or deliver you Your Awesome Life. To do this to yourself is self-sabotage. It's the fastest way to feel frozen with fear, out of control, and numb with overwhelm.

Constant self-analysis of your so-called defects is never going to bring you closer to your Centered Self.

And the more you focus on yourself, what's wrong with you, what you need to "fix" and what's not working, the more miserable, insecure, and uncertain you will become.

So the "game" is this – your Guardian wants you to stay "safe," and it interprets this as you doing as little as possible to risk anything, ever, for the rest of your life. Ideally, if you could stay home and watch old reruns on TV, that would be epic.

But there's this whole other part of you – Your Centered Self – who's crying out to be heard, and needs a better PR person, frankly, because she doesn't have the best message in comparison. Your Centered Self is saying: "Get Out There and live! You're worth it! You've got this! Go you!"

See the difference? The message of Your Centered Self requires… well… *action*. It needs that you do the opposite of what your Guardian thinks and believes you're really comfortable doing. It requires that you be vulnerable and face your fears. And figure out what you love. It's really scary, revealing, I-don't-know-if-I-have-what-this-takes stuff.

And it never stops.

Crap.

It's at this point in my workshops that I remind people I'm not a motivational speaker full of all kinds of spin. No one seems to argue with that.

And my cheery message continues. I'm not saying you don't have flaws. We all do. At different times in my life, I've been overly selfish, self-absorbed, felt obsessively sorry for myself, was depressed for no reason, was unkind, harsh, critical, judgmental… and I made myself feel sad and lonely because of these defects. And then I made myself even sadder and lonelier thinking about how sad and lonely I was because of my flaws…

None of this brought me closer to knowing myself, liking myself, or feeling great about my life.

Neither My Amazing Life nor Your Amazing Life can ever be the recipient of endless self-criticism.

There is nothing wrong with reflecting on an aspect of yourself that you think you can improve upon, and then figuring out and learning how to do just that.

The problem comes when you get stuck in first gear – "What's wrong with me?" "Why me?" "Why can't I just… ?" – and you don't shift gears.

Live life with the expectation that your full participation will resolve much of what bothers you

Much of what bothers you about yourself is learned conditioning from your past. It's automatic self-criticism that you picked up as you grew up. You don't know yet how to see yourself differently. This quest you're on will resolve this for you, not because you're reading these pages, but because you will bring the pages to life with your own experiences.

And you have flaws.

That's being human.

And it's okay.

The message here is to **live full-time *despite* your flaws. Work on what you want to change *as* you live, not *so* you can live.**

If you wait until you're "perfect," or "together," or "feeling confident enough," or "feeling the courage I need," you will never act.

Perfection is a myth that doesn't exist for anyone.

If you wait until your Guardian shuts up telling you to stop living, you will never live, because it will never stop.

No one has it together. No one. Not. One. Person. Some people are getting on with it, regardless.

The One Relationship You Need to Claim Your Courage

There is only one relationship you and I need to build to learn how to be courageous. If you change this one relationship, everything changes.

Just this one thing:

> *Teach yourself to become comfortable*
> *with making mistakes*

I'm saddened by how many people think they have a "procrastination" problem when what they really have is a terrible relationship with their own humanity. They will avoid anything – including the things they suspect they may love – to avoid the feeling of being revealed to be human. And most of the people who I see held by the throat by this fear are terrified, not by what *others* may think or say, but by what *they* might think and say to themselves.

I see people hiding. Making excuses. Pretending they're too busy. Cowering behind "busy family lives". Lying to themselves with the placatory "I'll do it later". Or they're declaring a very reasonable-sounding "fear of success / failure". In honest moments they're berating themselves about how small they're being, but doing their best to keep the show going with well-worn platitudes.

Trapped in the quicksand of their minds.

If you can't face your own humanity, then you can't face the fact that you are capable of making mistakes. You can't accept that you don't have all the answers, that you don't have it all together, that you're not completely confident all of the time. That you feel shame when you think about failing, and that you feel terrified by the very idea of being seen to fail, even by yourself. If this describes you, then you feel trapped in the cage you've built for yourself.

And yet, you're no different to *anyone else*. The whole of humanity – everyone – making mistakes. Overcoming setbacks. Facing challenges. Living while flawed. Sitting with this is not easy in the beginning. We've been taught to bounce away from what we feel is shame at the *thought* of making mistakes. But what if, instead of trying to avoid mistakes, you committed to accepting that you will make them and that to make them as you learn was *vital* and necessary for your journey to your Centered Self?

Challenge Your Conditioning

Here's an insight that was a wonderful source of comfort to me. If, when you grew up, you were shamed when you made a mistake, or you were mocked or felt outcast, you associated making mistakes with being emotionally abandoned. When I understood this, it was comforting to me because it informed me that my journey was never about me "getting it all together," but instead it was about me embracing my emotionality – to welcome, celebrate, acknowledge, own, and allow myself the experience of emotions that I had pushed away since childhood.

It doesn't really matter what the endeavor is. You could be a gun Wall Street super-stud who looks like you've got it completely and utterly made, and yet you can still have an irrational fear of abandonment, a fear of vulnerability, and of intimacy, and of emotional realism. My talking about all this is causing you discomfort.

Change the subject.

Please.

You can be a multi-millionaire property developer. A hippy, spiritual type. A teacher. A therapist. A "go with the flow" kinda guy. An uptight, buttoned-down analyst. A mother. A university lecturer. A mechanic. A homeless person. A celebrity. But none of these outside "suits" means spit when it comes to being able to live in your own skin as you face a setback, recognize your own mortality, allow yourself to feel vulnerable, learn, apply what you learn, and continue.

When you were growing up, the Big People in your life – to some extent or to a large extent – held tightly to their insecurities and then handed them to you. You didn't know that the flaw was in giving you their insecurities. A child doesn't have a choice but to accept their Big People's endowments. But you, as an empowered, centered adult, *have a choice.* You can continue to listen to the record in your head, which is your Big People's record that was given to you, or you can start to write a new one.

Start with some small questions as you work to develop trust in yourself. Is it true that you'll be rejected if you make a mistake when trying something new?

Is it *really* true? Or is it just what you've accepted as your fate, without really questioning it?

And is the person doing the "rejecting" someone who isn't supporting you?

May I ask why are you listening to them?

And have you considered that the person doing the "rejecting" is most likely *you*? Are you ready with handy put-downs, condemnation, and criticism if you make a mistake, so you hold yourself hostage from your dreams?

Don't be the hostage of yourself and rob yourself of your dreams; be daring and open to falling down so you can learn how to get back up and thus know you can handle it.

May I invite you to remember that you're capable of trying something new, making a mistake, and then learning from that mistake so you can do better.

You learned to walk.

You learned to ride a bike.

You learned to write your name.

If you drive, you learned that. If you catch the bus, you navigated that.

And in every one of these activities, you made mistakes along the way, learned from them, and did a little better the next time.

This lets you know that you can take small steps and teach yourself how to handle what comes up along the way. You've done it before. Take a moment and recall when you've had to dig deep within you to learn something, and you've made mistakes, learned more, applied what you learned, and then got on with it.

It's not what you were conditioned to believe in childhood that's going to make the difference *unless you let it*. It's your willingness to *overcome* the conditioning and to develop new, wonderful attitudes about learning and growth and your own humanity in making mistakes.

If you sit waiting until you "know enough," or feel confident enough before you act, then you're letting your fears drive your life, and that's not living.

Your quest to your Centered Self – just like in any great movie – is paved with mistakes, setbacks, unexpected twists and turns, breakthroughs, tragedies, and triumphs

The mess comes when you mistake your need to avoid the pain of making mistakes for an actual reason for not doing something. If the pathway to your own empowerment involves making mistakes – and it does – then make mistakes. Learn. Grow. Improve.

Recognize this universal aversion to feeling the shame of your own humanity. And then do what is not universal. Act anyway.

Recognize that if you feel the fear and still take action, you will earn your courage.

Take these three steps to take action in the face of your fear that you may get it wrong.

1. **Acknowledge to yourself that you're human.** You're not perfect. You're learning, you're progressing, and you're here today to be a little better than you were yesterday.

2. **Pick one thing you can do that will move you toward being a better version of You.** It can be the smallest thing, say, tidying up a room. Or it could be something more significant, such as applying for the job you want. This can be anything, but it's got to be something that you will do, not something you'd just wish you'd do.

3. **Do the thing as soon as you've made the commitment.** Ideally, do it within five seconds of committing to it. If it's a bigger thing, break it down and do the first, small step. Using the job application as an example – you've read the job ad, now write down where you think you're a match. That's the first step, and you've done it. You've done the first thing.

Let go of the energy that you waste in telling yourself you're no good, or telling yourself "Come on, just get on with it." Usually, it doesn't work. Instead, what it typically does is make you feel worse about yourself.

Just one small action step.

Right here.

Right now.

Accept That "They" Won't Change

Being empowered became important to me when I realized how much I relied on others. And not in a cool, I-know-how-to-ask-for-their-support kind of way. It was all about me being able to anticipate and predict *their* preferences and expectations. How *they'd* hurt me. How *they* might hurt me again. What *they* did to me in the past; what I had to do to get them to "like" me; and how to feel in control around them, so I wasn't judged by them.

I was buying into a bad script that said my life could only be shaped when others thought, felt, and behaved a certain way. And that "certain way" meant in a way that gave me a sense of control, certainty, and safety. For me, it was all about shutting down any form of "attack". Read: vulnerable moments, intimacy, people getting to see me as I really am, asking for support and then allowing the support.

It was a sad merry-go-round of who did what and what I would do about it to protect myself for next time. I would look for – no, I would *hunt out* – any form of fault or flaw in anyone I met. Better to get them before they got me, right?

But "they" weren't getting with the program. "They" were, no matter how much effort I put into it – and it was a lot – staying stubbornly free of my influence and manipulations.

This included my family, my friends, people I met, people I imagined I'd meet, and people I'd never meet but would fantasize about meeting. You get the idea. No one was free of the quick tally of flaws I'd do in my head as I assessed just how f*cked up they were compared to me.

If I could find enough flaws, that would free me not to have to feel bad about my own shortcomings. It gave me freedom from the responsibility of ever having to sort my own shit out, because, hey, have you seen how messed up *they* are?

Oh, the utter exhaustion of it all.

Two blindingly obvious ideas occurred to me Back Then. First, no one was responding as I thought they were supposed to. Which sucked. And no matter how hard I worked this particular angle, it wasn't – go figure – making me feel particularly empowered.

A third idea crept up on me, and then a fourth, which I quickly cast aside several times before finally giving them both my full attention. What if I stopped trying to get people to be a certain way? And what if I stopped looking for everyone's flaws?

The questions were awesome, I grant. My answers, not so much. I really couldn't see any other way to be with people except to be controlling and judgmental. I knew I was never going to empower myself with the way I was going about "relating," and yet alternate ways of relating were, to me, what I decided were "low return" strategies. Which meant, they didn't make me feel "safe".

Maybe you don't relate to this, and perhaps I'm the only freak in the room. Or you relate to your own version of this. However you got here, if you find yourself thinking that *they* have to change, or *they* have to do something to make it right, then I'm sure you've guessed where this is heading…

It's not *them*.

It's *you*.

No matter what they've done, or you've perceived they've done, waiting for them to change is only hurting you

When you wait for someone else to change as the reason why you're not doing what you need to be doing, you're really saying, "I have no power. This other person controls me."

Recognize that this belief says that something outside of you controls you; that someone else has sway over your choices, that you are dependent on another.

Know that you are the reason for how you feel, for what you think, and for how you live. You didn't have this power as a child. And now you do.

Use it.

It's clunky at first, as is anything unfamiliar. I remember having no clue about how to stop blaming my parents for feeling depressed until I realized one day that the only person hurting – was me. And then I had no clue what to do once I'd stopped blaming them! The difference was that now at least I was giving myself the opportunity to learn how to empower myself, instead of leaving my power with people who didn't even know they had it.

Be uncomfortable. Sit with the uncertainty. Stay with the feelings of inadequacy and of fear. Just sit with them and don't distract yourself with TV or busyness, or some excuse to avoid them. Just sit with the truth that "they" aren't going to change and even if they did, it wouldn't help you feel, think, or live differently. This is because the illusion was always that this power lay somewhere else other than with you.

The truth of the matter is that it's always been with you.

Remember, you are retraining your mind, so patience is called for. Be patient, but keep reading. We'll be turning these pages together.

You Are Awesome

You are awesome. You have the power to choose how you respond to life, your thoughts, your perceptions and your actions. You can, whenever you want, give yourself honest appraisal about how you're doing and where you need to lift your game. You are capable of committing to yourself and to Your Awesome Life. You're the catalyst for the change you want to see in your life.

Regardless of whatever flaws you have, you are free, right now, to embrace life.

You live life knowing that your full participation will resolve much of what bothers you.

You make mistakes. You learn. You grow. In fact, you know that to grow the mistakes are inevitable and required. You feel freedom within you because you can take on new challenges knowing you can handle whatever comes along.

And no one has to change for you to live your life.

This Matters So Much: Annette Sayers' Story

I spent twenty years trying to work out what was wrong with me.

Struggling as the single mother of a drug-addicted teenager and dealing with many addictions of my own… I felt lost, lonely, depressed, unworthy, unloved, and unlovable.

The funny thing is, so many people would say I was doing amazingly well and that I had created a great life for myself. Little did they know I never felt truly happy. Everything was a struggle, and I was exhausted from trying to please people, from playing the roles, and from putting everyone else and *their* needs before my own.

I was keeping "busy" and focused on what was Out There, because focusing on how *I* felt hurt too much.

If only I could get rid of some problematic situations in my life, I would be happy… If only my son would listen to me, life would be great… If only people in my life "got" me, all my problems would be solved… Clearly, I was way too focused on the external, without pausing to think – how could *I* bring about the change I so desperately needed?

I discovered Sharon's Ultimate You quite by chance. And my entire journey started to unfold, step by step, for the better, in front of my very eyes…

With the help of the Ultimate You Quest community, I made a decision to draw a line in the sand and I found the courage within to take full responsibility for what was happening in my life. I realized that I couldn't change other people – this was going to be an inside job.

To my surprise, after six weeks of me working through the Ultimate You Quest program, my family started to see a change. They asked me, "How are you doing that?"

Wow! I couldn't believe it… my internal work had started to be reflected in my External World.

The journey to my Centered Self has enabled me to connect with my deepest feelings, and my innermost needs and emotions, all of which I had been suppressing all these years. This has empowered me to finally resign from roles that didn't serve me and to find parts of myself that I never knew existed.

I'm slowly learning to set new boundaries and embrace the warrior within… I'm discovering how to connect with my own feelings and emotions and meet my needs resourcefully… I'm stepping into new territories, where I can now fully embrace myself for being me…

And I know I couldn't have done this alone. I've had so much support from the awesome Ultimate You Quest community, its amazing coaches and mentors – the change has been phenomenal!

This is the beginning of me, Annette, playing a bigger game and not hiding in shame anymore.

I am worthy.

I am lovable.

I am enough.

Key Messages

- Being empowered is what you deserve and is your natural state. Here you're free of thinking that "somehow and somewhere this all goes away and everything is fine."
- You, and only you, are responsible for your life. Joy comes in knowing you can handle this and that you're the leader of your own life.
- How do you the little things is how you do *everything*.
- It's up to you to be proactive about what you want to experience in your life.
- Your flaws can't be the focus of your thinking. Instead, live life with the expectation that your full participation in it will resolve much of what bothers you.
- Earn your courage. Don't hold yourself hostage by robbing yourself of your dreams.
- No matter what "they've" done, or you've perceived "they've" done, waiting for them to change is only hurting *you*.
- If you see obstacles as a "sign" that you shouldn't make proactive changes to your life, you'll never do anything worthwhile. Instead ask yourself if the path you're on is aligned with who you are and who you're becoming.
- Surrender the thinking that says "things" have to be easier before you'll do them. Instead, aim to be better.
- You must be your own source of healing.
- You are not the exception.

RESOURCES FOR YOUR JOURNEY

A companion worksheet, an exercise for you to do that relates to this section, a video from me, and more resources are available for you at:

www.ultimateyouquest.com/quest-support

CHAPTER 2

Your Second Gift:
Living a Conscious Life

*"Our beliefs create the kind of world we believe in.
We project our feelings, thoughts and attitudes onto the world.
I can create a different world by changing my belief about the
world. Our inner state creates the outer and not vice versa."*

John Bradshaw

Your second gift – living a conscious life – is to begin to choose, design, and create your thoughts so that they support you, champion you, and move you in the direction of Your Awesome Life.

In the coaching work that I do, a constant theme of my training events is the "automatic" living people don't even realize they've adopted – making decisions because they've always done things that way even though the decision hurts them or hinders them in some fashion – and how liberating it is when they wake up.

If you continue to let your thoughts, beliefs, choices, and behavior run on "automatic," without critical assessment of their effectiveness, you will feel diminished. You will feel depleted, even when you're rested. There may be a feeling of ill-at-ease within you. The more you delay taking care of your Truest Self, the more that your automatic reactions will feed the doubt gnawing away within you.

What happens when you drive your car with the handbrake on? No matter how you try to drive forward, you're being held back. It's the same when you set an intention to be more loving, or less critical, and then promptly slam on the brakes by falling into the same old habits that hurt you last time you were here.

Conscious living is releasing the handbrake and embracing the journey of discovering who you are under the layers of conditioning.

"A seagull never speaks back to the Council Flock, but it was Jonathan's voice raised. "Irresponsibility! My brothers!" he cried. "Who is more responsible than a gull who finds and follows a meaning, a higher purpose for life? For a thousand years we have scrabbled after fish heads, but now we have a reason to live – to learn, to discover, to be free! Give me one chance, let me show you what I've found…"

The flock might as well have been stone.

"The Brotherhood is broken," the gulls intoned together, and with one accord they solemnly closed their ears and turned their backs upon him."

Richard Bach, *Jonathan Livingston Seagull*

One of my favorite pastimes is to ponder on what type of world would I ideally like to live in. And then I ask myself whether or not my thoughts, my choices, and my behavior are consistent with my ideal.

So let me put that question to you:

What kind of world do you want to live in?

And what you want for the world… is it how you live your life?

Your second gift – to seek to live consciously – is not something that you'll receive; it's something to be noticed, cultivated, and encouraged within you.

What It Means to Live Consciously

Conscious living, to me, is you and I deliberately responding to life, rather than merely reacting to it as we previously have. It's understanding that the smallest moments shape your destiny: how you greet someone; whether you hold a grudge; how you support yourself in challenging times; how you care for your living space. All of these small moments add up to the sum total of your day, which becomes the sum total of your week, then your month, then your year, and finally your life.

Conscious living is when you recognize it all matters.

This does not happen by chance. It doesn't arrive just because enough time has passed. It's earned through the efforts and decisions you make each moment to move you toward your own empowered life.

Conscious living is you moving out of the automatic reactions that led you to repeat the same patterns of behavior over and over again. It's you embracing, with conscious choice, the path to your own Centered Self, even if it turns you away from the path you thought you were meant to be on.

- *You are aware of and in touch with the aspects of yourself that run on automatic,* and which debilitate you.
- *You consciously develop new ways of responding to your world around you,* which are aligned with your truest expression of yourself.
- *You're open to seeking new choices and new paths for the expression of your Centered Self.* Your mission is to seek to help your Centered Self find full expression.
- *You're comfortable with and embrace taking care of yourself with compassion and patience.*

To be unaware – to live automatically – is to live according to the conditioning of your past, without question or thought. It's to passively accept how things are and how you are an immovable object in that web of life. It's to hide from intimacy and vulnerability – because only through conscious living can you claim the courage needed for their expression.

Conscious living is the journey to discovering, embracing, accepting, loving, valuing, and restoring your Truest Self

Conscious living is to not need all the answers and to know that control is an illusion. This doesn't mean you are free of the need of control… it says you're aware of its seductive powers and that, daily, you practice to release yourself from its clutches.

It's to accept others with compassion and extend to them the dignity and kindness they sometimes don't seem to deserve or want. You do it for you, not for them. You know that being awake is to be responsible not for others, but for how you respond to them.

To live consciously is to recognize, cultivate, encourage, and cherish the notion that each of us seeks and deserves to live a life that's as true to our expression of ourselves as we possibly can be.

I don't believe this is achieved by randomly living your life however the wind takes you, or by wishing it to be so without some underpinning commitment and effort. To live consciously is most definitely earned because from what I've observed, it's not something we learned to seek for ourselves when we were growing up.

How "Automatic" is Your Life?

Consider the questions here and determine whether or not they apply to you. Some may seem contradictory for they're simply two sides to the same coin of running your life on "automatic". It will give you insight into where automatic living is extracting a toll on the quality of your life.

- How many times a day are you "triggered" or upset by something someone says or by a situation? Do you react the same or a similar way each time? Do you react to how this "makes" you feel? Do you believe people shouldn't "trigger" you or offend you?
- Do you try to control others by judging them, pointing out their flaws, or reminding them of their past or current failings? Do you feel tension within yourself if you don't get these ideas "off your chest"? Do you think people should do things your way? Do you believe you know what's best for others?
- How much time and energy do you put into proving that you're right? And making sure others know this?
- Do you "go with the flow" to avoid conflict or upsetting people? Do you hide what you really feel so you don't be a bother?
- Do you find yourself giving unconditionally to others, only to find your generosity not reciprocated?
- Do you feel stuck and powerless to do anything about what's going on, because "everything" you try seems to lead you back to the same stuck place?
- Do you have patterns of repeated outcomes that cause you pain in different areas of your life? Perhaps relationships? Your finances? Your career?

These are just a few of the ways that we can, without even realizing it, mess up a perfectly good life.

I think I've done all of them.

Let's Check Under the Hood

Everything that you perceive, think, feel, focus on, decide, do or don't do, changes your brain, whether you want it to or not.

What you attend to, focus on, think about, care about, worry about, obsess about becomes neurologically more prominent in your brain.

And equally significantly, what is locked and loaded in your mind as your way to react to situations – regardless of the effectiveness or non-effectiveness of that reaction – becomes your default reaction if you don't question it and take genuine steps to break the habit.

Your brain doesn't develop strong synapses (pathways to experiencing emotion) unless it sees a habit forming. What you do consistently is what will become wired into your neurology.

Connections that are less active will receive less nerve growth. They will deteriorate, like plants that don't receive water or fertilizer.

When an older, unused connection diminishes, space is freed up for something new to be planted.

Ruminating on your suffering, especially past suffering that you can't prevent because it's already happened, causes the brain to increasingly focus on suffering. You can train your brain to feel suffering, simply with practice.

The more you rely on the automatic reactions that are already embedded within your habitual brain circuits, the more you'll react automatically to new events, even if the reaction is denying you Your Awesome Life. The more you train your brain to go to the memory of some prior event, some experience, some hurt, the more easily your brain will get there. And faster. And more often.

This isn't about ignoring our past, and it's not about ignoring suffering. It's not about pretending everything is fine when it's not. It's recognizing that to live consciously you need to focus on what's within your power to change, by questioning your automatic reactions, and by cultivating the actions that will move you toward the life you want.

You can't live consciously if you keep thinking about your past.

You can't live consciously if you keep focusing on the past injustices done to you.

You can't live consciously if you continuously make the same poor decisions that prevent you from living Your Awesome Life.

Instead, you will become miserable. And feel like a victim. And feel sorry for yourself. It won't get you a great life. It can't and it never will.

Whatever you focus on becomes neurologically strong;
you can reshape your brain to respond naturally
to whatever you want it to

However you're wired right now, know that you have a choice about how you will be wired tomorrow. If you want Your Awesome Life, learn the wiring for its attainment.

Trapped By a Story

The natives in Borneo have an ingenious way of catching the wild monkeys that raid their food supplies. They make a small hole in an empty coconut shell. The hole is just big enough for a monkey's hand to fit into. Rice is then poured into the coconut shell to use as bait, and the shell is then tied to the ground. The monkey smells the food, investigates, sticks his hand into the coconut shell to grab the rice, and then tries to remove his hand.

In grabbing the rice, he's made a fist with his hand, but he can't pull the fist out of the hole, so it's trapped.

To escape, of course, the monkey has only to release the rice. But the monkey won't do this. He holds onto it, trapped by his own behavior.

We all have stories about what's wrong with us, our life, and the world. Your story may be about your relationships, or your career, your health, your wealth or lack of it, or your family – any place that you feel stuck, frustrated, or defeated.

Your stories are what you tell yourself about why you can't have something, do something, or experience something

It's the stuff you've convinced yourself is true, without really questioning or challenging it. It's the unconscious bias you have towards an area of your life that you accept without question.

Stories often come from your past and from your tribe of origin. Perhaps you experienced an upsetting event when you were younger. You saw an aspect of your parents that left you feeling overwhelmed or undervalued. Whenever your brain experiences the sensation of fight or flight, it creates stronger memories than it does when recalling the good times. Disturbing experiences are "chemically supercharged" and stay with you longer and more strongly than pleasant memories do.

I like the way Marci Shimoff, world-renowned transformational teacher, puts it… It seems our brains have Velcro when it comes to the unpleasant stuff, and Teflon when it comes to the good stuff.

The key is to wake up and recognize that you are in charge of your mind, and not the other way around, and you get to decide what your mind feeds you. Just know that it wants to persist with the stories because that's how it's been trained to act. It needed to protect you, years ago, from too much overwhelm, or from feeling unvalued, or from feeling afraid. To do this, it went into "protection overdrive", giving you more and more reasons why you shouldn't risk yourself or your tender feelings. It did this to keep you safe when you couldn't protect yourself.

But now you can protect yourself. Your brain doesn't know this, because you've let it run the show. It's doing what it learned to do and now doesn't know how to let go, support you, or champion your desire to live a conscious life filled with compassion, passion, love, and joy. In reality, it finds those notions pretty confronting and terrifying.

The campaign to "take back your mind" is probably the most vital campaign you'll ever engage in

You're literally going to wrestle with your mind because it's been trained to reject change. It's going to turn up the excuses and the justifications because it thinks the best thing to do no matter how miserable you are is to play it safe, stay small, and don't change.

The You who is awake, aware, and willing to take back your mind, knows better. You know the best thing for you to do is to dump the stories you've been telling yourself about why you can't, and replace them with consciously designed stories that allow for positive outcomes. You know the best gift you can give yourself is to begin to treat yourself with kindness, compassion, tenderness, and respect.

- What's your story? What do you tell yourself over and over again about why an area of your life isn't the way you want it to be? How do you justify the pain you feel? The disconnect?
- Is the story you tell yourself true? Really? Completely, 100 percent true? Is there any of it that is, perhaps, a little "enhanced," which keeps you in victim mode, so you don't create change?
- What would happen if you dumped the story and replaced it with a story that your Centered Self just loves? What if, instead of reminding yourself of all the reasons you can't, you find at least as many reasons why you can? What if, instead of avoiding an adventure, and comforting yourself with a story of how it wouldn't have worked out anyway, you have the adventure? Consider the different expressions of yourself that may become available to you if you freed yourself from the need to conform to a construct you've kept in your head for too long.

Get your hand out of the coconut shell and let go of the story that has become your prison!

Don't Believe Everything You Think

My self-talk used to go around and around in circles, touching on all of the well-tested tropes that were guaranteed to drag me into fear, self-doubt, and paralysis.

I'm not good enough.

What's wrong with me?

Why can't things just go my way?

I will just fail; it's easier if I don't bother.

It's too hard; I can't do it.

Who do I think I am?

And so it went, these same thoughts, bouncing around in my head all day, every day, mixed with hours of thinking the sky was about to fall in and seeing the worst in every situation.

The more I practiced this self-talk, the more it felt like the truth, and the more I believed it. I was in a stupor of self-doubt and immersed in my own poison 24/7.

According to scientists, each of us has approximately 60,000 thoughts each day, and 95 percent of these thoughts are the same thoughts, over and over again – day after day, year after year, playing the same record on repeat. It's like you have a playlist of music, and then you play the same tune on shuffle all day, every day.

And if you're anything like most people, 80 percent of those thoughts are negative and don't help you nurture the flame within. That's 45,000 negative thoughts. Every day. Of every week. Of every month. Of every year.

These negative thoughts then stimulate the areas of the brain that are associated with depression and anxiety.

Consider how many of the thoughts you have in a day empower you. How many, by comparison, just run through your brain on automatic, because they've never been questioned?

Your thoughts aren't always true, so
don't believe everything you think!

Centered people know this and have trained their mind to work for them, instead of against them.

You can do the same!

Start by becoming skeptical about what you think, especially the negative thoughts that just seem to run on automatic pilot.

Ask yourself if the thought is really true. Then ask yourself three questions:

1. How am I hiding by telling myself this?
2. Who would I be if this thought was not true?
3. What would I do if this thought was not true?

You're introducing new "programming" into your brain so that the old programming gets a little upgrade. Picture the Matrix, where Neo gets upgrades into his thinking so he can conquer the next challenge. You're giving yourself the much-needed boost to your thinking that your brain can't give itself.

The Wolf You Feed

One evening an old Cherokee told his grandson about a battle that goes on inside of people.

He said, "My son, the battle is between two 'wolves' inside us all.

One is evil. It is anger, envy, jealousy, sorrow, regret, greed, arrogance, self-pity, guilt, resentment, inferiority, lies, false pride, superiority, and ego.

The other is good. It is joy, peace, love, hope, serenity, humility, kindness, benevolence, empathy, generosity, truth, compassion, and faith."

The grandson thought about it for a minute and then asked his grandfather: "Which wolf wins?"

The old Cherokee replied simply, "The one you feed."

You have a built-in tendency to register the negative more strongly than the positive. Because of this, you may be feeding the wrong wolf. To live consciously and with awareness, your Centered Self needs you to even things out a little bit.

Wake up to the positive moments and experience them
more deeply and with conscious thought

To do this:

- Choose a moment you enjoyed. Think about how it was positive. Feel the joy of it being a positive experience. It doesn't have to be a seismic event. It could be merely reading this page as you sip green tea with the sun on your face. Allow yourself to notice the warmth of the sun. Give yourself permission to acknowledge yourself for giving yourself the time to read and sip tea. Let the mundane be wonderful, notice it, acknowledge it, and enjoy it.
- Keep doing this throughout the day, day after day, until your brain learns that you want it to bring your attention to what's wonderful in your day.

Don't be the person who thinks "I'll be happy when…" This is only teaching your brain to delay ever feeling joy. The goalposts move, and joy is never felt.

Instead, seek and appreciate the smallest moments and consciously cultivate appreciation for them. It takes practice, sure. But so what? Give yourself thirty days of quiet appreciation – pause to appreciate the small moments – and share your appreciation each day with someone in your life.

If you're thinking this isn't worth your time, do it anyway.

We'll meet at the end of thirty days and compare notes.

Are You a Puppet?

Back Then, I wanted to live my best life, and feel that I was in the driver's seat in my own mind. Yet I came to realize I was locked into ways of thinking that seemed automatic, beyond my control, and self-sabotaging. It was as if invisible forces pulled at my life. I was a puppet and had no idea who or what held the strings.

I came to view my puppet strings as two opposing ideas in my mind, which had, I'm sad to say, replaced me actually thinking about my life with any real depth.

One of the strings was this idea that everything had to be under control. And when I didn't feel in control, I had to get everything around me – and everyone around me – under control.

I must have been a real blast to be around.

The other string was the opposite idea and was more difficult to touch. It was as if I couldn't risk offending anyone, or risk disapproval, or have anyone reject me.

Which is a weird conflict of strings. On the one hand, I wanted people to comply with my version of reality, which I suspected they didn't like. And on the other hand, I wanted everyone to not disapprove of me. And I think it's worse than that. I guess in some warped way I was trying to get people to see the world my way so they would comply, and because of that, they would then like me.

Yup. That's genius. Can't believe it didn't work.

I came to recognize these two opposing forces as rigidity and permeability. Both of them were me running on automatic, and I barely gave them any real thought. But so entrenched they were, I believed everyone should see the calm logic of this mindset.

Rigidity and permeability: two sides of the same coin

For some things, like how to get dressed, how to prepare a meal, and how to get organized, running on automatic was a great thing. It saved me having to think about every damn thing I had to do in a day. I'd learned how to read and write. I didn't need to relearn this skill every single day, which saved hours and hours of relearning and rediscovering and reinventing.

But I noticed I went into "automatic puppet mode" for some stuff in my life that warranted a little more thought – like how to have a meaningful, emotionally intimate conversation, for instance. I sucked at this. I would get self-conscious without even trying, worry that I sounded "bad," look desperately for any clues from the other person about how I "should" be, and then try to become this. I did it over and over and over and over again. I could see myself doing it. I could hear the words I was saying. I could feel what I was feeling. And yet I had no mechanism for hitting the much-needed "stop" button and evaluating any of it.

I'm pretty sure I lived in pain every day but remained utterly convinced I was on the right track.

The String of Rigidity

Have you ever just been locked into a way of doing something that you haven't questioned?

Like it just has to be this way, even though, well, that's bullshit.

This rigidity is the inflexibility you may have over how something must be, no matter what it is; no matter how big or how small.

When it's for the little things – like how to set the table – then it's probably not going to create too many challenges in your life or set you up for too many tumbles. But when it involves the more significant things – like negotiating relationships, raising children, making decisions about your career, or your beliefs about how everyone should behave – then it's... well, problematic.

Let's say you fall head over heels, could it ever have been this great, best-thing-ever in love. Then you find out he's cheated on you and you're in ruins. You promise yourself you will never go for that type of guy again.

And then you do.

Sigh.

What is the matter with me?

Or perhaps without any conscious thought, you test people before you let them get too close to you. Even if they pass the test, you can't let them get too close because really, they still might betray you, and then –

They do.

And you are left with the thought: I know I can only count on myself, dammit.

Or your kids are old enough to learn for themselves, do for themselves, think for themselves, and you're still hovering over them like an umbrella on a rainy day. They don't develop crucial social skills, vital resilience, or essential confidence because their moves are smothered by you. You know on some level that you're helicoptering, and yet you still do it.

Don't tell me how to raise my kids!

Or you try to stop yourself, but you find yourself prioritizing housework and the need to have a clean house ahead of having fun with your family. You're the clean-freak perfectionist who insists that you're installing "discipline" in your kids, even though you suspect this is more about your issues around control than it is about the mental health of your family.

Hey, I love my kids! Don't go there.

Or perhaps people aren't allowed to disagree with you without you getting defensive or aggressive – sometimes both. Anyone who disagrees with you is your enemy and has betrayed you.

They had no right.

Or it could be that you defend a status quo just because that's the way it's always been. You put "tradition" and "history" ahead of new ideas and ways of approaching something. You're on a team, and you're the person everyone else has to work around.

Don't tell me my business. I've been doing this longer than you've been born.

There are millions of examples of rigidity at play in the world. I'd like to invite you to consider where this may be in your life.

- Look for where the patterns of behavior repeat themselves, over and over without question because *That's how it's always been,* or *That's just how it is.* You may hear the words… *Do as I say* or *Don't you dare question me.*
- Or look for where the results of a decision you've recently made may have been eclipsed by circumstances or changing conditions, yet you still continue to make the same choice day in and day out, even though it's clearly out of step with reality. No one feels empowered. Instead, there's righteousness and defensiveness and uptightness; pursed lips and hard hearts prevail.

This rigidity comes from unquestioned habits that have developed over a lifetime. For many of us, to question them is to commit a sin. The toxicity is in the rigidity.

I remember that when I questioned my dad, I was treated as if I'd poked a sacred cow.

Don't go there.

The ensuing toxic rigidity means that it's become an immovable slug of an idea that perpetuates simply because it does. There is no justification for it, except *That's how we do things around here.*

You may be familiar with some of these: *Don't you raise your voice to me… It's not my fault there are no good men… Why does this always happen to me?.. It's just who I am… What does she want from me? I work hard, don't I? I provide for them. Isn't that something?*

It's as if the blinkers are on, locked in place, and to remove them and see the matter from a broader perspective is just too much to ask. And it is, in a way. To face our own fears head-on means to confront the raw and the real stuff of our lives, which is something most of us have never been equipped to do. I'd go further and say that most of us have been actively discouraged from facing our own defenses.

It's when you see yourself shutting down intimacy. Vulnerability. Compassion. Softness. Thoughtfulness. Because to access these traits within you causes inexplicable fear. Which you deny. And call "weakness". Instead, you offer platitudes, make a joke, offer distracting alternatives, or change the subject. You act like you've got it together and that the other person is making too much of a fuss. This isn't your problem. In short, you do anything and everything to avoid having to face your feelings of inadequacy in a vulnerable moment.

There's nothing to see here. Move along.

Back Then, I recognized I was running on automatic with a big dollop of rigidity thrown in for good measure. In these time-worn instances, I believed I was right just because that's what I had always thought was right. That was, sadly, as far as my thinking on the topic went.

But then one day I asked myself, *"What if you're wrong?"*

Thirty-seven years... And the dawning realization that this righteousness, defensiveness, and rigidity was all utter rubbish.

The String of Permeability

Have you ever swung completely the other way from rigidity, and literally not had a view about something that really matters, only to realize later that your lack of a response reflects a habit of not wanting to offend anyone, or upset anyone, or deal with the confrontation that might ensue if you really spoke your mind?

For me, this occurred with a family member who is very aggressively defensive. Easily offended. In the past when I'd encountered this response from them, I would go with the flow, not assert myself, and not rock the proverbial boat. This meant that my needs were secondary, rarely considered, and often belittled. Tiring, to say the least.

This is the automation we create and maintain in our lives by being permeable. Here, avoiding our own feelings of anxiety are more critical than our boundaries, our needs or our sense of what matters.

So, what's the problem? Isn't being nice, being agreeable, so damn... lovely?

On the surface, yes. Except doormats exist for a reason.

In this scenario, everything is a democracy, and nothing gets decided because no one wants to cause offense or upset anyone else. You can't say that. I'm offended.

It's the indecisiveness that comes from never knowing what you stand for or believe in because to take a position may alienate someone. I'll just go with the flow. Whatever.

It's the loss of faith that results because no one is accountable and no one will take the moral responsibility needed at the moment. Hey, be cool. If they want to do that, let them.

It's the boisterous, out-of-control toddler running through the crowded restaurant with the parent smiling and nodding and watching like it's their own home and everyone should love and tolerate their child as much as they do. Hey, I'm just letting my child be free.

It's the naïve hope that no one will hurt you. You just put your faith in whoever shows the slightest interest in you because if you show you're trusting, they will honor this and not take advantage of it. Won't they? Why won't anyone see how good a person I am?

It's the super-helpful person who becomes a martyr by ensuring that everyone else's needs are attended to. Then they secretly wonder: When does anyone do anything for me? They hide the confusion that results when no one does, or they post on Facebook how they think perhaps they should get away from everyone because everyone is so damn selfish. Hey, I'm a good person. It's everyone else that just uses me.

It's the person who agrees to do something and repeatedly lets you down, and then promises they won't do it again. Then they do it again, and you keep putting up with it. I don't want to make a fuss. They're so busy. I don't want to be a bother.

This don't-rock-the-boat behavior of yours seems so innocuous. So innocent. So all-inclusive. So compassionate. It's not. Compassion is smothered in this environment where there are no limits, no one can say "no" without hurting someone's feelings, and no one has any clearly defined sense of themselves.

It's a world where every feeling, thought, perception and belief has an equal voice, even unthought-out, lazy or self-serving ideas. It's a world where a half-baked view holds equal weight with the view of a qualified expert. Where feelings are mistaken for facts. Where to question is to offend.

And the antidote:

Full frontal self-appraisal with a hefty dose of
"the world doesn't pander to you and your sentimental ideas
about how the world should be"

And this just isn't, in my experience, a popular or well-received idea. It's hard to give up our sentimentality because the alternative – facing the facts as they are – is really, really challenging.

Again, as with rigidity, most of us have been actively discouraged from ever facing the limits of our own inept attempts to construct a reality that just doesn't exist anywhere.

And despite its self-proclaimed embracing of love and inclusion, and I hope I didn't upset you and don't you worry about me heroics, it chokes out vulnerability. How can you open up to someone who can't even see a harsh reality for what it is? How can you have a serious conversation about your fears when you're met with the self-conscious need to be liked?

Automatic Behavior Hides Your Lack of Trust

Both flavors of surface-skimming living – rigidity and permeability – suffer from a massive dose of shallow thinking. Understandably. Nearly all of us have been raised to not look too closely at our patterns of choice and behavior.

And we need to scrape away the easy-to-toss-around platitudes and see that underneath there is something insidiously ineffective with either extreme when dealing with the realities of the human experience.

Ignore it. I'm just going to live my life. It will go away.

But it doesn't.

And that's the thing about either rigidity or permeability – they hate the light. They hate to be questioned. Because under the justifications and explanations and excuses, all you're left with is:

I feel unworthy.
I feel unlovable.
I feel that I'm not enough.
I can't reveal my insecurities to you (I can't even reveal them to myself).
I don't know how to trust.
Please don't hurt me.
I do this to prevent you from abandoning me.
I have learned to defend against judgment.

Both versions of automatic thinking are really shields against not knowing what to do about being hurt, judged, mocked, rejected, abandoned, or shamed. But it's more than this. It's not knowing that you can handle any of these scenarios.

It's:

I don't trust me with what will happen if I leave the script.

I know what happens when I stay on script. I may not like all of it, but I know it. And that's comforting. If I leave the script, I don't know what will happen next. And I don't know that I can handle it. I don't know that I can trust me with that level of unknown.

And because few people are taught how to trust themselves, it's easier to, and makes more sense to, just run on automatic – and suppress, ignore, deny, or reject the painful truth of our own emotional frailty.

The Need for Order

On some level, we do what works, or we wouldn't do it. Even when we do things that seem to be hurting us or holding us back, our original intentions are positive. So whichever version of automatic thinking and behaving you lean towards, you're seeking – as we all do – to impose order on chaos. You're trying to feel okay.

It makes complete sense to do this. You may not have even realized that you were running important parts of your life, which needed conscious thought, on automatic pilot. And if you did know, it's highly unlikely you've been taught how to handle this tendency of allowing your reactions and responses to life to be on automatic. Because your Big People were doing it, too – jeez, they were the people who taught you how to do it!

I was absolutely committed to living My Awesome Life. It's just what I was doing to go about achieving this fell far short of being what was needed to accomplish it. I was out of my depth and paddling in the wrong direction.

Apparently, you can't be righteous and correct people all the time and make friends. Who knew?

Apparently, you can't pretend to have it all together and be falling apart inside, and live a great life.

Shit.

Apparently, you can't live in fear of being "found out" to be a fraud and still feel authentically whole.

Hmmm.

Apparently, you can't judge everyone and not get blowback that affects your own self-esteem.

Arghhh…

Apparently, you can't stay rigidly the same while waiting for everyone else to change.

Apparently, you can't be a human pinball, never share your needs, and never put your needs first, and feel self-love.

All of these are examples of how I ran my life on automatic, expecting somehow, finally, that it would all work out, despite the ineffectuality of what I did. And even though on some level I could sense that I was the common denominator in every experience and situation that went south, I didn't see in sharp focus how much my ineffectiveness was messing up my life. I placed the need for certainty way ahead of my need to learn how to approach my life and myself in a radically different fashion.

My need to impose order over chaos dominated, at my expense.

And this exists at all types of levels and is everywhere you look.

This can manifest as chaos in your personal life. You may have experienced the same woeful fitness, personal care, relationship, or financial reality for far too long, allowing your choices in these areas to be made automatically rather than giving it thought.

This can also manifest as family and relationship chaos. One person wants something different from the group, another is not conforming to expectations, another is acting like the family isn't crucial, and this offends another person. No one pulls up from the crash that's coming because everyone is reacting by way of their automatic programming. It's like a sad dance. You say one thing, which everyone knows will set the other family member off just so, which leads to this other family member stepping in to placate everyone, which drives another family member trying to dispel the tension with humor, which annoys this other family member who thinks everything should be handled without fuss. And so it goes… everyone experiencing familiar chaos, which passes for order, as everyone settles for "at least it's familiar".

This can also be chaos across a community: How we respond to marriage equality, how we respond to changing educational needs, how we respond to the changes that are needed in religious institutions. One group rejects the status quo with no thought to consequences. Another group is hostile to any talk of change, believing it's "offensive" to even think about it. All play their roles like well-trained marionettes. There's no real discussion. Nothing productive comes of it. And everyone is walled up and in their bunkers by the end of the first hour.

At whatever level you enter the narrative, you're faced with players who operate with distrust at one extreme or the other – yet both extremes playing from the place of rigidity, dogma, and blind allegiance to their rules.

Neither extreme is fully geared for the conversation because both are coming from a place handicapped by lack of insight. One extreme is marked by a lack of willingness to see that quoting doctrine and claiming "that's how it's always been" is not always the answer. The other is the too-enthusiastic willingness to "just do something," or trust "karma," or "no one can be offended when we talk" with no sense of personal responsibility or accountability. Both sides of the coin keep the conversation shallow, so that there isn't too much uncertainty, because uncertainty leads to chaos.

And chaos, for so many people, signifies a fundamental lack of self-trust.

The Third Path: Showing Up

I'd like to suggest that there is a third pathway – one where it becomes possible for you and me to upgrade our approach, our perspective, and our choices so that we are able to handle the uncertainty we encounter when we leave the automatic way of being behind and feel a sense of self-trust as we do it.

I can't tell you it's the most popular path. Too many people have an aversion to thinking at a deeper level. To challenge someone's thinking can be synonymous with questioning their very identity. We may even feel consumed with shame when we challenge our own thinking in any real way.

It's as if "I think you can do better than this" becomes the same as "I'm attacking and confronting you because you suck". One statement is radically different from the other, but the recipient of the comment automatically goes on the defensive. There isn't a lot of latitude for honest discourse about our Awesome Life if the default position when receiving feedback or new ideas is to lock down in the bunker and prepare for war.

With that said I don't imagine you're reading this to be told that "everything is great, carry on, don't change a thing".

Let me just set the scene a little more here. What I'm going to suggest requires a lot more thought of a deeper kind, a desire to have a stronger sense of yourself, a willingness to be wrong, a desire to seek new and more efficient pathways forward, and an ability to be vulnerable enough to admit when you don't have an answer.

No more platitudes.

No more blaming "them".

Okay, I need to get to the real point here.

The alternative I suggest is:

Be willing to assess the moment,
the experience, the conversation,
and the decision for its merits

It's to be present to what is, rather than what you expect, prefer, or want.

It requires us to set aside the ludicrous and delusional notion that we always know what's best, that we are always right, that we are always in control (hilarious!/not), or that we have nothing to learn.

It insists that instead of deciding the world must match our beliefs or we're unhappy, we attempt to see the world for the way it is.

It takes courage and a willingness to really ponder the dynamics of any given situation. It also requires playfulness and openness and vulnerability. It requires the ability to be intimate with our own limits of thinking in such a way to open new pathways of possibility. In being open to new alternatives, maybe we do move the dial a little closer to Our Awesome Life.

Let's call this third path **"Showing Up"**. The early indications you're doing this will be discomfort, a desire to shut that shit down, a complete lack of certainty about what to say or do next, and, if you're anything like me, a conviction that you're doing it all wrong.

I believe it's a monumentally giant leap in your consciousness when you show up, not to control things, or "win", or dominate, or ingratiate, or be liked, or not piss people off; but show up instead to be fully present to what is.

People who are living automatically won't get you or will feel very uncomfortable around you. They will most likely complain about how you've changed (and you have). They will even try to keep you on the train tracks that you used to run on.

And you will, my God, let yourself down, forget, make a mess of things, and flounder.

Sounds awesome, right? I know. Let's just forget this and go see a movie or something.

And yet doesn't something deep inside you, no matter how hard you fight it, tell you you're a lot more than a derailed train?

Okay, if you're still with me, here are some thoughts on how to know when you're showing up and not hiding out:

1. **Adjust your response to allow for the different, unfamiliar and perhaps vulnerable**. That means if you were rigid about a topic yesterday, today you look at what others think about it. From this expanded perspective you learn, adjust, and quite possibly change your previous views. You stop defending the status quo and instead look very carefully at what would give you maximum movement towards Your Awesome Life.

   When it comes to being in relationships with others, you give up defending how they have to be. You give them the freedom to be who they really are, and you accept that, for in doing so you are giving them Their Awesome Lives.

   And if you were permeable about something yesterday, today stop dodging responsibility for this area of your life and own it. Because that matters. You showing up in this moment matters. It matters more than anything. To keep showing up like you can't impact the outcome is to say, "I don't matter. I have no worth." That is not okay. It's not helpful. And it's not true.

2. **Stop lying.** To yourself. To others. Just stop. I know we talked about this in discussion about the first gift, but there's no escaping its significance on the quality of your life. Tell the truth to yourself about what you're doing, and especially about what you're not doing. Don't beat around the bush. Don't placate yourself with nice

reassurances. Don't let yourself off the hook by saying "I'll do it later." Stop the lying and just say the truth.

3. Instead of saying something to shut a conversation down, **encourage others to open up**. You welcome the conversation, the different ideas, the opportunity to learn. You know that shutting down a conversation is about your discomfort, right? You will feel uncomfortable in kicking open these doors, and I know from experience that you will, very possibly and very literally, squirm. But suck it up. Stay with it. You will see very rapidly that the automatic program you were running helped you avoid any form of intimacy with anyone. That is so incredibly sad and totally unnecessary.

4. **Come through when you need to** – for the little things and for the big things. It doesn't matter if it's inconvenient, you don't want to do it, or you've changed your mind. You said you'd do it. You do it. You become remarkably predictable for others so that they can trust you. You own that when you let others down, you're telling yourself you lack self-worth.

5. Change your relationship with mistakes and setbacks. **Dump the bullshit automatic aversion to being human.** You will make mistakes. It's inevitable. The only way to avoid mistakes, or avoid setbacks, is to do nothing, say nothing, and stand for absolutely nothing. Now if you've already tried doing this and you noticed how miserable you felt, you can now face your humanity and see you've been making a mistake all this time.

6. **Be present to what is, and not what you'd prefer it to be.** Embrace this moment for what it is. Experience it fully, as it is. Set aside your self-talk telling you your preferences and your expectations. Let this moment be.

It's seeking to understand, rather than always needing to be understood

It's seeing how intimate moments, vulnerable moments, precious moments, cherished moments, aren't created from a defensive posture, but from one of openness, warmth, love, availability, and thoughtfulness.

Your Awesome Life is held fragilely in the hands of your willingness to show up.

The Red Pill

To live consciously does, on occasion, become a mental wrestling match. You will inevitably vacillate between what you think you know but don't know, what you know you don't know, and what you think you don't know and probably need to learn a little bit about.

And sometimes you'll remember how much easier it was when you didn't know and didn't know you didn't know.

But you've taken the red pill, Morpheus.

After this, there is no turning back.

You take the blue pill – the story ends. You wake up in your bed and believe whatever you want to believe.

You take the red pill – you stay in Wonderland, and I show you how deep the rabbit hole goes.

Now we both know that conscious living is recognizing that energy is wasted wishing for things to be different, or for someone to change, or for "things" to be easier.

This Matters So Much: Jodie Hunter's Story

Eighteen months ago my life was in turmoil.

I was angry at everything and my heart was sad. I had left an unhealthy relationship that myself and my partner had created and there were moments that I had this unrealistic fear that I'd end up homeless and not be able to support myself. My life had become an unhappy, anxiety ridden, anger-fueled habit. For the last few years I had switched on autopilot and the desire in me grew to make a change.

I would listen intently every time Sharon shared her ideas for Ultimate You as she was writing this book… The message triggered something in me more than any message I had heard in a long time. The more I listened, the more I knew that it was time to do something for me, to make a decision… and more importantly… make a change.

And I am so grateful I said "yes" to Ultimate You… because that's exactly what happened. I have made a change. A lot of them!

I started the journey of shifting from unconscious living to conscious living and I committed to it 100%. Every day I woke up and re-committed to do the work. I knew I had to stop hiding and bring myself out of the shadows. No more being in denial about how I really felt and pretending to be happy instead. It was time for me to start acknowledging my pain and allowing myself to feel it. It was time to learn about being compassionate to myself.

It was time to claim my life.

I started to learn how to stop reacting to everything around me and start consciously choosing my responses. I started asking…"What would love do here?" I learned how to feel my feelings and know that was okay. And the biggest part of all, I learned to take responsibility for me, my thoughts, my feelings, my actions, and allowed others to take responsibility for theirs!

To say everything has changed is an understatement.

Personally… I have learned that I matter, that my needs matter. I have learned to trust myself, and that it's ok to be uncertain and not have the answer for everything right now. The most beautiful part is I have learned to love myself, and because of that I now have close and beautiful friends in my life who I cherish. Professionally… in the last year I have made and saved more money through my business than I have in any other year in my entire life. I went from having thoughts of not being able to support myself to creating the best financial results in my life. And this is just the beginning.

Being me is f*king awesome! I haven't felt this way for forty-seven years!

This isn't just another book or just another online program.

This is a life-changing journey…

Key Messages

- Conscious living is you moving out of the automatic reactions that lead you to repeat the same patterns of behavior over and over. Now you embrace – with conscious choice – the path to your own Centered Self.
- Your brain is a bunch of wiring, and you can shape your thoughts based on what you focus on.
- To feel constant disappointment, sadness, worry, or anger is not being free to feel whatever you want. Instead, you're addicted to these emotions, and trapped by them.
- You must challenge your old, stuck beliefs that tell you why you can't be someone, have something, or change something.
- Start all change with small steps that you can manage and see yourself doing.
- Rigidity and permeability equal toxicity. The status quo that you defend, which doesn't bring you joy, is the pain in your life. It's the conditioning you haven't questioned yet.
- Conscious living is to be open, curious, and willing to discover and explore new ways of approaching your relationship with yourself and with others.
- No matter how much you're used to undermining yourself, you can handle what comes along.
- It's not about how "things" are. It's about you and how you show up for what's going on in your life.
- Persist so you can learn who you are, and admire that person. Show yourself you're a person of self-worth.
- Self-respect is an outward-focused, perpetually renewing form of love that's not dependent on anything or anyone anymore.

RESOURCES FOR YOUR JOURNEY

A companion worksheet, an exercise for you to do that relates to this section, a video from me, and more resources are available for you at:

www.ultimateyouquest.com/quest-support

.

CHAPTER 3

Your Third Gift:
Freedom from Your Tribal Cycle

"Our greatest human adventure is the evolution of consciousness. We are in this life to enlarge the soul, liberate the spirit, and light up the brain."

Tom Robbins

To restore your Centered Self is, I think, a pretty extraordinary journey to undertake. You face your fears, your flaws – you have them, and so do I – and your insecurities. You encounter doubts about whether or not change is even possible. You contend with the "helpful" suggestions of others who mean well, or don't – but they have suggestions anyway.

Along the way, you deal with the unconscious programming from your past and do your best to shake off the automatic reactions that come with it. You face ingrained habits. And you wrestle with the uncertainty of not even knowing if what you're changing will lead to Your Awesome Life.

And to add to this pile of tough stuff, I'm going to ask you to dig a little deeper, hang on a little tighter, and lean in a little closer. Because you are now going to make a claim for your freedom.

If being open, curious, adventurous, nondefensive, and present is the foundation for Our Awesome Life, why don't you and I just *be* those things? Surely it would make perfect sense to act in a way that's consistent with our own best interests? Are we crazy not to do so?

Or maybe there's a bigger tractor beam keeping us pinned to our version of reality.

Cue foreboding music.

Along with your biology, your psychology, and the myriad experiences you were exposed to when you were growing up – your schooling, your community, your culture, the messages from your media – there is what I call your "Tribal Cycle".

Your Tribal Cycle

Your "tribe" is your family of origin, and the patterns of thought and behavior that your family engaged in represents your Tribal Cycle. The tribe is the epicenter of what impacted you, shaped you, and carried you into adulthood.

Your tribe had impactful individuals within it who shaped and influenced your thoughts, feelings, perceptions, and beliefs about the world. These are the "Big People". They may have been both of your parents or a particular parent, a foster parent, a sibling, a teacher, a priest, a friend. It could be anyone who touched, impacted, and substantially shaped your thoughts and feelings. The events and experiences you had with them, either positive or negative, interacted with, collided with, shaped, and informed who you were coming to believe you were, and from this genesis, who you are today.

How your parents were raised is influenced by how *their* parents raised *them*, which is influenced by how *their* parents raised *them*, and so on. So your Tribal Cycle is the perpetual repetition of patterns of perception, beliefs, expectations, choices, behaviors, and communication styles – good or bad – down through the generations.

All this becomes messy when the members of your family haven't been able to cope with intense feelings or conflicts, or if they don't know how to encourage or respect your boundaries. When stressed, your Big People were likely to have fallen back into learned ways of dealing with situations that were more about them managing their anxiety or insecurities rather than with what you, as a child, needed.

Wherever your family sat on this spectrum between "shut down" and "rocky-verging-on-insane", the members sought, unconsciously, to achieve their version of balance

Regardless of whether you were raised within a family that could best be described as "barely functional" or highly functional, the goal was balance and stability and the reduction of tension. For one person not to fulfill their part within your tribe to achieve this balance was to rock the entire tribe because the stability of the family was the primary concern.

The more adaptable, in tune, and present to you and your needs your tribe was capable of being, the less you felt the need to help maintain this balance.

The more insecure your tribe was, the harder you felt you needed to work for this balance. And if you and I can just unpack this a little more… The relationships the most influential Big People in your life had with one another determined the character of this balance – and the more pain they were in, *the harder you had to work to help achieve the balance overall.*

If your Big People were close and intimate and knew how to meet their individual needs on their own, you had less of a need to step in and "help".

If your Big People were distant, angry, accusatory, despairing, distressed, in pain, shaming, or displayed any other form of not being vulnerable, the greater you felt the need to step in and "help" protect your tribal system.

And the more your Big People attempted to get their needs met through you and/or your siblings, the more entrenched within your tribe you became.

No matter who you are, how you were raised, or what you believe to be true about how you were raised, you grew up in a family whose entire field of energy impacted every single member of your family. Attitudes become encoded within family members and then acted out in the family and society as a whole.

Your family, or the group that was considered your tribe, was greater than the sum of its parts

All this, and you were a *child.*

Try that on. You were a child. Trying to figure out which way was up. Shoelaces and making your bed were monumental hurdles for you to conquer. One of the Big People in your life communicated, either implicitly or explicitly, their lack of adaptability, through shut down emotions, perhaps through inconsistent love and affection, through making unrealistic demands on you, through pouring love, focus and attention onto you when what you needed was space to be your own person, or maybe by refusing to give you comfort when you needed it. Or they refused to discuss topics that made them uncomfortable, or they demonstrated a fundamental lack of respect towards their partner or perhaps made inappropriate demands on you or your siblings…

When it's good, it's great. When it's not, it's a sad and bewildering, sand-shifting-under-your-feet kind of experience, especially when you're a child. The dysfunction may have manifested in any number of ways:

- You may have been forced to "take sides" during conflicts between your Big People.
- Perhaps you, your thoughts, your feelings, your perceptions, and/or your views were ignored, criticized, mocked, minimalized, disregarded, or shamed.
- Your Big People may have been intrusive and overly involved and protective of you when you were ready to explore your world solo.

- Or they may have gone the other way, being distant and uninvolved.
- You may have experienced the crazy-making situation where your Big People contradicted your version of recent family events, invalidating what you knew to be true.
- You may have experienced violence or witnessed it.
- You may have been a "favorite," or not been a "favorite," or perhaps you were compared unjustly to someone else.
- Or perhaps you learned to be watchful and hyper-vigilant to the moods and expectations of your Big People, so you could anticipate and prepare yourself for what happened next.

You were a child who, through an innate and entirely normal and appropriate desire to survive, not be rejected, not be alienated, and not be shamed, tried your best to help this tribe and these Big People achieve some form of equilibrium.

Can you possibly imagine the strain this placed on your capacity for reasoning? For making sense of it all? You, like all children, would have adapted as best you could to what conditions you found yourself in, in a way that provided balance and symmetry to the relationships.

But, I have to ask, at what cost?

None of this was planned. It wasn't intended by the Big People in your life. It wasn't intended by previous generations. It wasn't intended by you. Perhaps you "acted out" – rebelled; or "acted in" – you harmed yourself or you were compliant. You did what you needed to do to survive and remain accepted within your tribe.

This isn't about blame. It's not about how "they" have to change before you will. That would be self-defeating.

This is the family system at play. And your Big People were as caught up in it as you were.

I believe that the number one block to our own well-being is the extent to which we don't recognize or acknowledge that we're caught in our Tribal Cycle

You may have wonderful habits that you learned from your tribe, and these are a significant part of your Tribal Cycle. You may have pretty awful patterns of behavior, too, and these are also part of your Tribal Cycle. If you've ever felt inexplicable anxiety about making a step forward in your life, it's because your proposed growth will take you out of the Tribal Cycle of your own family.

Sometimes the line between your Tribal Cycle and a behavior isn't always clear. I tend to make it simple for myself. If I'm doing something that keeps tripping me up, despite my knowing "better", then I'm probably caught up in some aspect of my Tribal Cycle. Instead of dealing head-on with whatever messed up pattern of behavior I've got going on, I check in with my Inner World.

Am I living my values, or am I trying to please someone else? Am I acting based on what I want to create, or am I acting out against an aspect of my Tribal Cycle? Am I choosing the path for My Awesome Life, or am I playing out the next generation of my Tribal Cycle?

It's time to make the invisible visible. To pull from the darkness the hidden pressures upon you to be and to act a certain way.

The Dynamics of a Healthy, Functional Family

When things are humming along in a functional family, each member recognizes that everyone else has different thoughts, feelings, perceptions, and preferences. They are comfortable with the fact that each person can make independent decisions and they recognize that those decisions may impact each other.

In these relationships, one person can see how someone else is upset but doesn't get caught up in that person's emotions, thus avoiding escalating the situation through "taking on" the emotion.

One person can make a decision to do something that sits outside what is considered "the norm", and it's registered as being "different and okay".

The need to make the family look good isn't there. You make decisions because you believe they move you and your life forward, rather than wave the family flag in distress.

You can be heroic when you believe it's needed, or lighthearted, or objective, or emotional. Then, in the next experience, you can be contrary to any of these responses, depending on what you believe is appropriate for you and the situation. You, and how you show up, is not limited to a fixed, expected role whose purpose is to maintain the family's balance. Each member of this family can move between different roles without consequence. There is a free expression of you, and for each member of the family as well.

You grew up free to express yourself as you are. The balance between individuality and being a part of this family was achieved without judgment and without anyone trying to get you to "conform" or fit in when you stepped outside of the group. You didn't and don't have to give up being you for the sake of the family's expectations.

Conflict can be handled without passive-aggressive tactics, manipulation, silent treatment, or the "punishment" of those who rebel. It's handled with direct communication of each person's needs and emotions. A desire to understand the other is the norm.

The leaders – the Big People – in this family don't see their children as existing to reassure them, or remind them that they're "good parents". If you were a child in this family, you weren't there to make them look good through compliance or rebellion.

You could feel what you felt, and label it without feeling isolated, rejected, or judged. And you could express how you felt without shame because all emotions were treated with respect.

In this scenario, there is reciprocity of care, respect, and love. This doesn't have to be demanded. You *give* care, respect, and love. You *receive* care, respect, and love. You don't have to "earn" it through performance. There are no conditions. And it's not withdrawn by you or anyone else when someone makes a mistake or hurts someone else's feelings.

Your Big People didn't think they had all the answers but still gave you the guidance you needed to flourish into your version of You. When they made a mistake, they apologized. When they made their stuff about you, they owned it.

And each of you have a sense of self that's grounded in self-worth. You know you're enough. You know you can handle it. You don't expect life to become easier. You simply improve on the You that you were the day before.

Enmeshment

Enmeshment is when any number of people interact with a lack of awareness of or consideration for each other's personal boundaries. Boundaries are permeable, unclear, and often ignored; or are rigid, unyielding, and impervious to emotional intimacy. Enmeshed families are rigid systems that become locked in over time, and it can be a tough gig to break out of these established patterns and roles.

In this environment, it's challenging to develop emotional and psychological maturity.

Whatever challenges you have, either from your childhood or in your adulthood, they are an "SOS" about your Big People's pain.

Your symptoms of pain are a message –
a message that you are distorting your own growth
in an attempt to try to alleviate and absorb
your Big People's pain

And as you, an adult, attempt to "find your own way" and "forge your own life" you are, in effect, trying to change the whole tribal system's way of operating. Your attempts at expanding your life and choices – your moves toward your own well-being – are a threat to the contracted and inflexible ethos of your tribe.

If you feel that life seems to get harder and relationships seem to fail to live up to their promise, you are apt to become frustrated, lost, alone, and in pain. This is you stumbling upon the discovery, perhaps years after leaving the tribal home, that you're still entrenched in the "job" you had as a child.

You learned your job as a child: maintain the status quo regardless of its lack of health, at all costs. And this you did, but you didn't do it consciously, or with conscious thought about its consequences to you. Again, how could you?

The greater the entanglement, or "enmeshment" you have with your tribe, the harder it is to have your own life. And the easier it is to repeat patterns of distress, such as procrastination, self-sabotage, addiction, repetition of the same mistakes, lack of intimacy, feelings of loneliness, anxiety, perfectionism, anger, sadness, not trusting others, constant disappointment…

Specifically, you may notice that you experience some or all of these challenges:

1. You may have an exaggerated sense of responsibility for others; or you are often in conflict and rebellious.
2. You feel guilty when you take care of yourself; or you can't function unless being cared for.
3. You have few self-determined goals and often wonder what your "purpose" is.
4. You have difficulty knowing or expressing your needs.
5. You have trouble knowing what appropriate boundaries are.
6. You struggle to distinguish between feeling and thinking.
7. You function in reaction to others.
8. You lack beliefs or convictions of your own about who you are, and how you want to shape your life.
9. You're unclear what a close, emotionally intimate relationship looks like or what it takes to achieve one.
10. You repeat patterns of behavior which cause you pain, or you keep experiencing the same relationship mistakes.

The lower the self-esteem and sense of self-worth your Big People had, the greater the enmeshment, as they attempted – unknowingly – to become lovable, worthy, and enough through how they engaged with you and what they demanded of you.

I was raised with love, and my parents did the best they could for our family. We were what you would call a "normal" family. My parents conceived me before their marriage. This was a big deal in the sixties (yes, that long ago!). They were too young, confused, and had little support. Years later, at my birthday parties and special events that were supposed to be in my honor, all the guests were told with humor about how I was a "mistake". A poem was written about this hilarious "mistake" for my eighteenth birthday party and read to all of my friends.

It wasn't funny to me. I didn't mind that I'd been conceived before my parents were married. I did mind that occasions that were supposed to celebrate me turned into occasions to make fun of me. To mock me.

I protested a little bit, and was told it was all in good fun, and that I should "lighten up". (God, how I came to resent that "advice!") It didn't occur to me to just say no. This is probably because I felt that I had no power in the relationship to voice my hurt and have it be taken seriously.

I questioned my own sense of self as I worried about my hurt. Yes, I worried about what was wrong with me for feeling hurt. How crazy is *that*?!

At some level, I guess I sensed that treating the situation with humor mattered to my Big People. I put their needs ahead of my own. I played the role of the well-behaved daughter and smiled through the poem as it was being read.

My relationship with my parents has matured since then. Healthy boundaries are becoming more normal for us. Expressing our needs is possible. It's new territory for us and we're closer than we ever were when I was growing up. But "Back Then," we were enmeshed.

You become enmeshed when your feelings, thoughts, perceptions, and ideas are treated as secondary by your tribe. You – the You you're becoming – is set aside for the you that the other family members want to continue to see. The traits of Your Centered Self – lovable, worthy, fierce, determined, passionate, compassionate, sensitive, emotional, expressive, creative, opinionated, loving, warm, curious, adventurous – are discouraged, or worse, are shamed.

You set aside your Centered Self and learned to "play the game" of being who your Big People needed you to be. And the extent that you felt you needed to do this is the extent to which you remain enmeshed today.

Your claim to freedom begins when you are free of the enmeshment. It's to embrace the You that you were meant to be, before the conditioning set in to tell you otherwise.

The Twelve Rules That Enmeshed You

If any (or all) of the following were your perception of your upbringing, then you're entangled or enmeshed (the two terms are interchangeable). None of this had to be explicitly said. It wasn't necessarily spelled out that *this is how it would be around here*. It could have been sensed by you, or perhaps you saw how a sibling was treated and that taught you how you needed to be.

You are enmeshed if you're still preoccupied with disappointing the Big People, including yourself

In thinking about all of this and mulling over the family dynamics that you grew up with, you may not remember a particular event or anything specific. It may simply be a sense of how it was in your tribe, and the rules that governed it.

The Rules:

1. You get to feel what the Big People are comfortable with you feeling.
2. You get to think what the Big People are comfortable with you thinking.
3. You are here for the Big People, to fulfill their need for security and reassurance.
4. You will be praised for achievement, not for effort or improvement, or just for the You that is uniquely You.
5. You learn not to talk about a topic unless the Big People want you to.
6. The Big People can criticize you, and get impatient and angry, and you can't.
7. Don't ever make the Big People look bad.
8. Mistakes are shameful and to be avoided.
9. If the Big People are uncomfortable by your behavior, you have to stop. You aren't here to make them feel uncomfortable or challenged.
10. There's a right way and a wrong way, and you have to get it right.
11. When you're wrong, or you fail, the Big People can reject you.
12. The Big People don't have to change, you do.

You may have experienced being belittled, criticized, or punished when you made a mistake. This would have set you up to fear mistakes, so you came to fear learning, and now you fear new experiences. You may have decided it's easier not to try because the price for getting it wrong just isn't worth it. Or you may act like you don't care and convince yourself of your indifference. Or you become a super-achiever. All are versions of being entangled and *still living out your reaction* to the expectations you took onboard when you were a child.

Perhaps you were denied feeling the anger of injustice when you were blamed for something you didn't do. Or you weren't listened to by your Big People as you attempted to articulate your feelings of rage. This denial translates into your enmeshment with your tribe, for you lost your sense of yourself and questioned your own sanity. You were sure you felt mad. Then you were told that you couldn't feel that. And then you were told off for feeling it anyway.

You may have been smothered with love and closeness just when developmentally you were ready to take some tentative steps towards your own version of You. The steps didn't happen. Or became a warped hybrid of who you are supposed to be and who your Big People want you to be.

Crazy-making.

And the Big People are never to blame. Children internalize everything and believe it's all *their* fault. So you blamed yourself for feeling "wrong" and now, as an adult, you feel unsure of yourself.

Insecure.

Untrusting.

Any wonder?

Groundwork to Get You Un-enmeshed

You and I will do some groundwork right now in preparation for becoming un-enmeshed. Then the rest of the book will guide you towards Your Awesome Life, adding building block after building block to your own Centered Self.

Let's start by acknowledging that you're enmeshed. (If you recognized your family of origin in the twelve rules, then you're enmeshed.)

Your tribe had a hold over you that may still be strong today. I would go further and say that the more enmeshed you are with your tribe, the less you can move towards the joy, compassion, creativity, and openness that's available to you when you have a sense of your own well-being. Your Centered Self is not present to you when you're enmeshed, because your Centered Self is not enmeshed.

You can't become yourself until you stop trying to live in reaction to the way that you were expected to behave when you were a child. This includes unconscious, automatic habits that are holding you back, which frustrate you and you wish you could change.

You must un-enmesh from the Big People until you don't see them as all-seeing, as all-knowing, as "right," as the arbitrators of your life, as the deciders of your fate. And this includes the Big People who aren't in your tribe.

Maybe you're reading this and saying to yourself that you don't see your Big People that way anymore and that you know they're not perfect, and that they made mistakes, and that they acted out their own insecurities on you. I'd say it's great that consciously you've recognized this. And then I'd ask if you feel a sense of well-being and live in a way that's aligned with your best interests and the best interests of others you are close to. Are you joyful? Free of fear? Compassionate to yourself and others? Adaptable to circumstance? Do you embrace mistakes with the knowledge that they're as essential to you as any creative endeavor?

Do you have relationships that are rich in texture and where emotional intimacy is easily expressed, enjoyed, and experienced without self-consciousness? Because I'd like to suggest that the unconscious, automatic patterns of choice and behavior you're running on are the best indicators of just how far away – or not – you've been able to move from your Tribal Cycle.

Most people have not moved very far away from their conditioned reactions of childhood. I have been in countless coaching conversations with an adult, but in reality, we're addressing the fears and insecurities of their child selves.

Unless we've made a very deliberate effort to face ourselves and see ourselves accurately and honestly – and this is not easy to do (and wow are there more pleasant ways to spend your time than holding a mirror up to yourself, warts and all!) – we're entangled with the echoes of our past.

"They" Aren't Changing

On top of all of this, your Big People aren't going to change. They may not even see a reason to change. They may not believe they are *able* to change. They may think everything is great as it is. And they may derive a smug sense of importance and control from things staying as they are. It might be, to them, that any change on your part, even as an adult, is threatening to them. They may go further and be completely against you changing in *any* way.

But don't discuss it with them. You aren't going to try to "win them over" and get them to agree with what you're doing. You're doing it for you – not for their approval.

You must be willing to take responsibility for You. This is your life. This is your decision. "They" won't make it for you. They can't. They don't even know there is a decision to make.

Does this mean the family dynamics may be challenged?

Yes.

Does this mean some family members won't "love" you as much?

Yes.

Will it be challenging?

Yes.

Give yourself the permission you need to see that you can no longer worship your parents; or, if you went in the other direction from them, continue to rebel. Again, remember, it's not what you've consciously decided about them. It's about the patterns of thought and behavior that you exhibit that point you in the direction of the answer to the question: "Am I enmeshed?"

Whatever happened to you, was not because of you. It was because of the Tribal Cycle you were born into. Generations of the same rules, repeated, over and over again… Susan Forward, Ph.D., in her book, *Toxic Parents*, shares the following wonderful advice: "Responsiveness allows you to maintain your sense of self-worth, despite anything your parents may say about you. This is extremely rewarding. The thoughts and feelings about others no longer drag you into a pit of self-doubt. You will see all sorts of new options and choices in your dealings with other people because your perspective and your sense of reason are not being buried by emotions. Responsiveness can put back into your hands a good deal of your control over your life."

So let's do this…

Blaming Them Will Never Work

So what do you do?

Let go, as much as you can, of blaming "them" for whatever you believe hasn't happened for you, what you believe you were denied, what happened that shouldn't have happened, what you didn't receive, what you should have received…

You are not "showing them" by withholding love, you are not "teaching them a lesson," you are not "giving them a taste of their own medicine".

You are hurting people who only know hurt. They are in the same Tribal Cycle you're in.

And you're succeeding only in holding yourself back as you live with the goal of getting what you believe you deserve from them – more love, more care, more respect, more time, more attention. Whatever it is, it's not coming from them, and it's time, really and truly, and please believe me, to seek other avenues of closure. Perhaps you don't indulge in any of these retaliatory tactics. Or maybe you don't do it consciously. Great, move to the next step.

Just remember that what is in your way is not your family of origin.

It's the relationship you think you need to have with them.

For thirty days, no complaining about your family. Not to your partner. Not to your friends. Not to anyone. If you find yourself slipping into old habits of complaint, even with yourself, catch yourself if you can. Just notice how much your mind wants to replay the complaint rather than find a solution.

And then pause for a moment on the thought that you're here to be all you can be. That you're here to live Your Awesome Life. That you're here to reconnect with your Centered Self. That you're here to be You. And to do this, you're willing to break some pretty ordinary habits.

Good on you.

Next, let's look at that little culprit of emotional reactivity and see how it's implicated in all of this.

Emotional Reactivity

"Emotional reactivity" is when you connect in your mind that something external to you is the "cause" of a feeling of anxiety, or panic, or negative self-talk. I can remember my dad saying when I was young, "Tone it down, Sharon." I felt such resentment when I was told this because I felt I was just being myself. I know for years after, when I was told this by someone, I would feel uptight, resentful, and rejected.

If you find yourself always going back to events from your past and feeling negative emotions when you do, this is also emotional reactivity. The goal is to be able to visit *any* experience from your past and be neutral about it, or better yet, not feel the need to visit it except to use it to draw on what you've learned so that you may improve the experience of *this* moment.

If you feel emotional reactivity around too many things, or too often, or if you think you're super-sensitive to what you perceive as criticism, even when someone simply doesn't agree with you, then your ability to move forward, build rewarding relationships, feel joy, and express spontaneity is going to be hijacked.

How do we prevent this?

The next time you feel emotionally reactive:

- **Notice what "triggers" the emotional reactivity.**

- Next, **notice how you react to your own emotional reactivity.** Just observe you doing what you do. And then ask yourself, "Is this reaction moving me closer to My Awesome Life?"

- The next time you feel emotional reactivity, **pause**, and instead of your usual reaction, be at a complete loss as to how to react. This is how it will feel when your usual reaction is not an option. It will feel weird and stressful and like something is incomplete.

- Don't strike out at the person if you believe it's something they said. Instead, pause, or take a breath, or remind yourself that you're on a quest to Your Awesome Life, so it's time to do some things a little differently. Or stay still and hold the space, or feel the anxiety within you and just acknowledge it without distracting yourself with an outburst. Or say, "I feel a little stressed by this; I'm going to need a moment, thank you very much."

- **Mentally step back from the scene** as it unfolds and observe how anxiety – which becomes emotional reactivity as each person attempts to relieve their anxiety – triggers each person who's there. I call this **"tension tagging"**. One person's anxiety builds up. Without conscious awareness, they seek to relieve their tension. They become emotionally reactive, and "tag" someone with their own tension. This person is now "tagged" with tension. Their anxiety will build. They will tension tag someone else. You can watch this spread throughout the group.

- **Don't tension tag.** Sit with how you feel. Your anxiety will pass. You will be okay. Trying to relieve your own anxiety through tension tagging will only perpetuate the Tribal Cycle.

It's a challenge, sure. Some of this stuff feels so ingrained within us it's like digging out a fossil from clay. Bits flying everywhere. Nothing clearly visible. Clay clinging to your body. The desire to get rid of it.

Just remember, you have a goal, and you can attain it. The goal is to reduce the emotional reactivity within you.

It's not to have "reasons" for it – people, events, life don't have to change so that you don't experience emotional reactivity.

You have to change for you

Practice, practice, practice, small steps, each day, learning to respond – rather than react – with reflective thought, calm, and grace.

Compare Yourself

At the peak of my enmeshment, when I turned every perceived slight into a wound to be nursed along with my grievances, with bitter competitiveness I'd compare myself to other people. Maybe this isn't your flavor of pain, but hey, each to their own!

I'd look at someone, without really knowing much about them or their life, and decide that if they looked like they had it in any way together, that proved I was a complete and utter loser.

I was caught in a web of my own making, created with the lies I'd spun about who owed me an apology and with the memories I harbored about who had wronged me.

So tiring.

Such wasted energy.

I wasn't the fastest to catch on, but it did, eventually, dawn on me that I was only hurting myself with all of these comparisons. And given that I was only looking *in* on someone's life without really knowing them, how did I decide they were "ahead" of me in life?

If you constantly compare yourself to other people as I did, delete this useless energy-zapper from your repertoire, as I did. You'll be much more at peace if you do.

Be your own benchmark of how you're doing
at this thing called "life"

Aim to take one step, each and every day, to improve yourself and your life. If an improvement on yesterday is for you to get to work on time, then that's a good start. Start somewhere. It doesn't have to be a big thing. In fact, no big things, please! No grand and sweeping gestures. No grand proclamations that this time will be different. No thirty-second dashes of activity.

Small. Consistent. Sustainable. Improvements.

For yourself. For the self you're becoming.

Don't tell your family of origin.

Definitely don't try to impress them.

The idea is to learn that you can impress yourself. Because as long as you think you have to get external validation, you remain the child, seeking approval, attention, love – for what you do rather than who you are. And to become who you are, you need to take action for yourself, without the applause, or the acknowledgment, or even – if your tribe is wired this way – the disapproval.

Just you.

Your Sweet Spot

Getting un-enmeshed is a fine line between *I have to please them, or at least not get their disapproval,* and *I want to be my own person, let me be.*

Belonging. Differentiation. Two sides of one coin. In conflict often. Sometimes in balance. Often in flux.

Sometimes just f*cked.

My dad wanted his version of what was best for me. He wanted me to be a lawyer. When, at the end of my first year of university I said I wasn't going to take the place I was offered, he hung up on me and wouldn't speak to me for two weeks. That's how it was done Back Then. Silent treatment. Withdrawal of affection to get compliance.

I didn't study law. And based on who I am, and how I now know me to be, I'm understating it when I say that was a very sound decision for such a messed up young woman.

But even if it wasn't a sound decision and I should have studied law, the point isn't who was right or who won the argument or what the "good" thing to do was.

I risked losing his affection, attention, and love by turning down that offer. I put my desire for *something else but I have no idea what it is yet* ahead of his need for me to make the family look good. I differentiated myself from my tribe and did not do what was expected of me.

Your un-enmeshment takes place not in theory, and not in your telling your original family how things are going to be around here from now on. It takes place in the moments in which you make a conscious decision to differentiate yourself, or you make the conscious decision to fit in within the tribe. It's not constant rebellion. It's not constant acquiescence. It's not in pitched battles for dominance. It's not in secret manipulations. It's not in lectures handed out to show how much you've got your shit together compared to them. It's not in cutting someone out of your life – although that is an option if your expression of differentiation is met with constant derision, anger, or shame-directed put-downs.

Differentiation in action:

1. Learn to **observe your family without becoming emotionally reactive**. Learn how the dynamics play out and the role you play in all of it.

2. **Practice being calm in the face of the emotional reactivity** of your family members. Observe, with compassion, how your own emotional reactivity is present, and just sit with it.

3. **Notice how the less differentiated someone in your tribe is, the more anxiety they have** and the less they're able to take care of themselves. They soak up anxiety from the tribe easily.

4. The more you differentiate yourself, the more anxiety will be triggered throughout your tribe. The less tolerant they will become.

5. The more differentiated you become, the more you'll notice you enjoy a network of emotionally supportive relationships away from your tribe.

6. **Don't attempt to "make" someone in your tribe change.** The work you're doing is for *your* differentiation of self. Pointing out someone else's flaws, blaming someone, being righteous, thinking you know best for someone else, or nagging someone are examples of your own enmeshment, not differentiation.

7. Notice that when you move to differentiate yourself from your tribe, they will exert pressure on you to be absorbed back into the status quo. You may begin to exercise, and your tribe doesn't value self-care, for example. They will react to this new choice with scorn, indifference, silence, distancing themselves from you, or some other version of tension tagging.

8. **Be mindful to the difference between a "feeling" reaction and a thoughtful response**. Automatic, emotional reactions are designed to relieve your own anxiety or the anxiety of another. Focus on sitting with your anxiety, not expressing it emotionally. Respond with the focus on your own capacity to see the perpetual drama unfolding, without contributing to the emotion needed for its continuation.

Sometimes you'll think, *Wow it's just easier to go to the family dinner than it is to argue with Mom about how I'm tired and just want to chill.* Sometimes you'll say, "Mom, I love you, thank you for the kind invitation. I appreciate it, and I'm going to catch up with you next week so I can just chill tonight."

You'll get unsolicited advice on your life (and you're in your forties), and you'll say, "Thanks for the advice. I know you love me and want the best for me." And then you'll do something that isn't advisable, according to your helpful family. Sometimes you'll follow their advice, and not as some random toss of the coin, either. You'll do it because you sometimes have to pick your battles, and sometimes you need to do what you believe is best for your truest expression of yourself. Regardless of the backlash.

There is always a fine line between how much of yourself you perceive you want to explore, and not suppress. Versus how much you want to fit in. And somewhere, in between these two choices, is your sweet spot.

If you keep disregarding what people think, you will feel disconnection. If you let yourself be defined by what people think, you become alert only to cues outside of yourself, stop trusting yourself, and lose touch with your own compassion.

The more you express your Truest Self, by exploring worlds away from the tribe and in ways that are interesting and hopefully life-enhancing for you, the more separate from your tribe you will feel and the more you will risk their disapproval. You can't control your tribe's reaction to your seeking to differentiate yourself. And I'll go further and say **if you *don't* receive pushback from your tribe, then you're not really differentiating yourself**.

Over time, people adjust to the changes being made by one of its members and will accept that member regardless. Some won't. If you're enmeshed and breaking free of your enmeshment, this will trouble you. However, as you become less enmeshed, you will recognize your own emotional maturity emerging and you know you'll be okay.

You're Worth It

How you traverse and explore the balance between belonging and individuality is your journey to Your Awesome Life.

The more you become aware of this and make conscious choices regarding this balance, the more flexibility you will develop. With more flexibility comes greater wisdom to see the moment accurately, rather than through the lens of "enmeshment" or "leave me alone". This wisdom frees you from pouring all your energy into the Tribal Cycle. Instead of thinking, feelings, fantasies, expectations, and actions being directed at others in your tribe, all that energy and focus can be directed towards Your Awesome Life.

It frees you to… live.

To achieve this, you need to develop a strong sense of self. A solid sense of who you are and what you care about. In Part Two… I Will Reclaim… we will do exactly this.

This Matters So Much: D'Anne Cowie's Story

I wish I knew then what I know now…

The impetus for change came when I was in a very dark place in my life, following the birth of my now eight-year-old son, Jesse. I vividly remember pushing him away just moments after he was born so I didn't have to touch him… I had been deeply shamed by my family for circumstances surrounding my pregnancy and I wondered how such a worthless person, as I felt at the time, could ever raise or have anything of any value to add to a child's life.

I was so emotionally shut down that I had no ability to feel anything for him when he was born. During the following year things went from bad to worse. This period saw me drinking way too much and the relationship with my son's father broke down as I entered a place where I truly believed Jesse, my beautiful boy, was better off without me in his life.

When I started working with Ultimate You, I started to understand what it truly means to take responsibility for myself, my past and my child. As I began to learn the tools to take back control of my life, I learnt a hugely valuable lesson:

Where we gift ourselves the space away from our dysfunctional family, to "un-enmesh", we can truly start to heal and rediscover who we are. It was in this space that I was able to become the person and mother my son truly deserves, and love him for who he is without handing on our families baton of dysfunction and unconsciously placing my unmet needs on him.

This program taught me how to find true forgiveness, love, and compassion for the past, for my family, and most importantly, for myself. I now choose to surround myself with people who love and appreciate me for who I really am and whose values are aligned with mine.

Breaking the Tribal Cycle is the biggest gift we can ever give to ourselves and to our children…

I'm forever grateful to Sharon and the Ultimate You.

Key Messages

- Your freedom is held within knowing that you can be vulnerable with others; you've embraced aspects of yourself that you've denied for too long; you trust your Inner World; you know you can trust yourself; you are free of absolutism; there is reciprocity in your relationships.
- Your "tribe" is your family of origin. It's the epicenter of what impacted you, shaped you, and carried you into adulthood.
- Your "Tribal Cycle" is the perpetual repetition of patterns of perception, beliefs, expectations, choices, behaviors, and communication styles down through the generations.
- "Enmeshment" is when any number of people interact with a lack of awareness of, or consideration for, each other's personal boundaries.
- Your symptoms of pain are a message that you're distorting your own growth in an attempt to try to alleviate and absorb the pain of your Big People.
- There are twelve rules that create enmeshment; they center around your feelings, thoughts, and perceptions not having been respected and nurtured.
- "They" won't change. It's up to you to reclaim You.
- There's no point in blaming anyone for anything. Everyone is enmeshed until they are aware of it and do the work to become un-enmeshed.
- Focus on your own emotional reactivity and work toward becoming less "triggered" by people or your past.
- Be mindful of "tension tagging" and the need to relieve your own anxiety through "tagging" someone else.
- "Differentiation" is balanced with connection.

RESOURCES FOR YOUR JOURNEY

A companion worksheet, an exercise for you to do that relates to this section, a video from me, and more resources are available for you at:

www.ultimateyouquest.com/quest-support

PART II

"I Will Reclaim"

To me, Part I is about waking up. It's about holding onto the truth that you and I are the creators of our world, and that we must be conscious about how we are creating our own reality. With this, we can untangle ourselves from what has hurt us and held us back.

With this in place and percolating within, let's go on to build on this in Part II, and discover the three foundation stones of you getting to know You.

If you find yourself not prioritizing yourself, people-pleasing, trying to fit in while denying your own needs, suppressing or ignoring emotions such as sadness, feeling like life is supposed to be… bigger than it is… then this second part of the journey will guide you back to your Centered Self. You will begin to get to know yourself.

We're going to be diving into the rich landscape of the Self-Esteem Triad – the triad that binds your sense of yourself. It contains the dynamics of your inner strength, how you show up for yourself, and how you may become emotionally intimate with the You that you were meant to be.

Your Self-Esteem Triad is where your boundaries meet and unite to give you a strong, grounded, and undeniable sense of who you are. This invisible force field around you tells you what's okay and what's not. It articulates your needs – what matters to you even when you neglect these needs – and your access to your emotional intimacy, where deep connection with yourself and others is paramount.

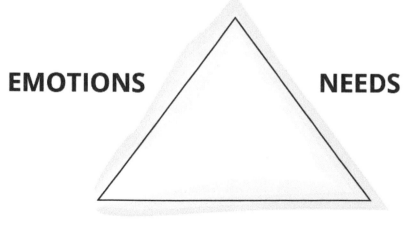

EMOTIONS   **NEEDS**

BOUNDARIES

CHAPTER 4

Your Fourth Gift: Being Lovable to Yourself

"Daring to set boundaries is about having the courage to love ourselves, even when we risk disappointing others."

Brené Brown

Your fourth gift – being lovable to yourself – is within you right now. It requires that you accept that the person who will rescue you… is you! This is a gift that can't be given to you by anyone else.

Many of us equate being lovable with being able to please. We are on show. We have something to prove. We have conditioned ourselves to think that we must *earn* someone's love.

Others believe they're unlovable, and because what we think of ourselves becomes what we expect others to believe about us, we then go about seeking evidence of that truth by being harsh, unforgiving, and judgmental to others and to ourselves. It's automatic.

But this conditional type of love is not love. It's not us being loving toward ourselves.

> "When we fail to set boundaries and hold people accountable, we feel used and mistreated. This is why we sometimes attack who they are, which is far more hurtful than addressing a behavior or a choice. For our own sake, we need to understand that it's dangerous to our relationships and our well-being to get mired in shame and blame or to be full of self-righteous anger. It's also impossible to practice compassion from a place of resentment. If we're to practice acceptance and compassion, we need boundaries and accountability."

Brené Brown, *The Gifts of Imperfection*

I know you have long known that being lovable starts within yourself. It starts with you knowing how to be compassionate toward yourself – with knowing and recognizing what matters to you and daring to bring this to life.

And being lovable is not about getting the approval of others or avoiding their disapproval.

To be lovable is to have strong boundaries in place

Being lovable means accepting yourself.

You accept yourself when you disentangle yourself from others, recognizing your boundaries, and the boundaries of others clearly. It means that you stop seeking permission and approval from others (even people you don't know), and seek to rely on your own internal guidance instead.

What Being Lovable Looks Like

To *know you're lovable* is, I believe, to begin to build that "Inner World" that's so crucial for your Centered Self to flourish. It's to know yourself, know what you care about, know what you stand for. It's to be aware of and enjoy your thoughts, feelings, and perceptions. And there's more…

- Because you are secure with who you are, and who you're becoming, without permission from others, *experiences don't have to be controlled, manipulated, and suppressed.*
- *Your ability to say "no" is in place.*
- *You've developed physical boundaries and sexual boundaries to help you feel safe, and you are able to prioritize your decision-making process.* This is based on what you value and consider important and informs you as to who you can be vulnerable with and who you should avoid.
- *You know where you end and others begin*, and this frees you up to know that what you feel isn't what someone else feels, and what someone else thinks isn't what you necessarily think.
- *You know that when you make a mistake, it doesn't make you a mistake.*
- *You're compassionate with yourself* and supportive of your own endeavors. You enjoy adventures where you learn and grow and delight in the unexpected moments.
- When it matters, *you no longer suspend your preferences in deference to everyone else*. It matters because you know *you* matter.
- *You learn, explore, and think for yourself.*
- *You say what you mean. You mean what you say.* You stick to your word. You apologize if you don't, and rectify it.

How wonderful is it when your relationships are with people who are courageous enough and aware enough to be on the journey to restore their own Centered Self too? How delightful is it when you, knowing where you end and others begin, respect their thoughts, feelings, and perceptions – and they do the same for you!

How important is it that because you know who you are and what matters to you, you feel freedom?

So many people say "freedom" is what they want. Yet they neglect the very path that would give them this…

Healthy Boundaries Look Like…

I can remember being so unsure of myself Back Then that I would wait tensely to see what others thought about something before I would cautiously join the conversation. Or would go to the opposite extreme and try to dominate the conversation so people had to agree with me.

Yep, what a party.

I began to notice that other people didn't do this, and had a much richer and rewarding experience of life. I'll just mention that had you told me this was possible Back Then, I would have thought you had serious issues. *No one* could be like this. And if they were, they were faking it.

Here are some thoughts about what characterizes this mode of being in the world…

- *You see yourself accurately.* Not worse than you are, and not better than you are. Just *as* you are – and not all blurry through the lens of how you think everyone else sees you and perceives you.

- *You know who you are*, what you prefer, what your needs are, what you're interested in, and you express these preferences by way of the choices you make.

- *You do what you say you'll do*, even if the commitment is only to yourself.

- *You develop appropriate trust over time.* You're not overly trusting in the early stages of a relationship; nor do you hide behind walls of distrust.

- *You give and receive love, care, and respect consistently* and without having to be prompted.

- *You behave according to your own values* about what it means to you to be the person you want to be.

- *No one else gets to describe your reality* or dictate how you think or feel.

- *You know you're responsible for your own happiness.*

- *You weigh the consequences of your actions on yourself and on others.*

- *You don't try to control someone* or have power over them, and you don't let others do this to you.

- *You're able to notice with joy when someone expresses appropriate boundaries.*

- *You respect the generosity of others* when they are generous with you. You don't devalue or dismiss this. You don't take this for granted or think it's what you're "owed".

- *You help someone because you want to*, not because you feel emotionally blackmailed or bullied into it, or because you "have" to be seen to be a "good" person.

- *You tell the truth.* You're okay if someone doesn't like this.

- *You accept apologies*, but you recognize patterns of deceit, selfishness, and lack of thoughtfulness, and you respond by managing your own emotional reactivity, requesting respect, and if the relationship isn't close, creating appropriate emotional distance.

- *You are compassionate*, empathetic, and kind to others. This doesn't mean you're a people-pleaser.

- *You can hear ideas that are in opposition to your own* and be delighted by the differences and be willing to discuss them.

- *You can say "no"* in a way that isn't defensive or reflects your need for approval. You're okay with someone else saying "no" and you don't take it personally.

- *You express what you want without manipulation*, without responding with the "silent treatment," aggression, passive-aggressiveness, or innuendo.

- If someone compares you unfavorably to someone else *you're not defensive*, and you don't take it personally. You privately explain to them that being compared to someone else is hurtful. You say that you are who you are and that you would appreciate that they respect this.

- *You don't look for reasons to be sensitive or upset*, but instead, assume good faith behavior on the part of the people in your life. In this, you give others the benefit of the doubt.

- *You're okay putting yourself first*, and you don't feel unduly selfish doing so. You have people in your life who know this is healthy self-care.

- When someone in your life is deliberately rude, gossips about you, or tries to spoil your moments of celebration and *you ask them for their kindness* and don't get it, you adjust accordingly rather than letting it continue and feeling personally devastated as a result.

- *You don't assume you know what's going on for someone else.*

- *You don't assume someone has it "better" than you.* You know everyone has stuff going on, and that no one has it made. Everyone is deserving of your compassion.

- *You are able to recognize people who are "emotionally mature".* You see their capacity for calmness under pressure, their lack of a need for drama, and their willingness to be open yet able to say when they don't agree.

- *You're able to recognize emotionally unsafe people* who willingly shut down vulnerability, who are self-involved, who see things in terms of black and white, who mistake feelings for facts, and who wish for a different life or circumstance and do nothing to bring it about.

- *You're able to express your preferences* and insist upon them when it concerns you. Equally, you can go with the flow when it doesn't really concern you.

- *People can give you feedback* that you consider without hypersensitivity, and if it's sound, you act on it.

- *You express gratitude easily.*

- *You reciprocate warmth* and openness without the need to "test" others.

- *It's not all about you.* There is reciprocity in your relationships that are characterized by a flow of attention, energy, and focus depending on what's going on for both parties. You don't make it all about them all the time. Equally, you don't expect it to be about you all the time.

- If you have a family, your children don't have to fulfill a part of you that you don't know how to fulfill. You alone are responsible for how you feel, how you think, and what you do. *Your "stuff" is about you.*

- *You don't respond in anger or judgment* when your child or someone else makes a mistake because you know that's about you and would violate their boundaries. You take a time out, gather your thoughts, and respond with appropriateness to the situation. You recognize that your emotional reactivity is you making their humanity shameful.

- *You get that your kids are not responsible for your own emotional reactivity.* Ever. You won't confuse your boundaries with anyone else's boundaries, including and especially your children's.

- Because you have a strong sense of self, *you know you're okay*. This means that others aren't there to make you look good, or "hold up the family's good name," or in any way champion what you think matters. People in your life are there to fulfill their journey, not yours.
- *You don't shame anyone*, including your kids, in their moment of vulnerability.
- *You celebrate people's efforts*. With them and with other people.
- *You're no longer addicted to rescuing others* to feel good about yourself. In fact, you tend to avoid people who need constant rescuing, as you recognize this as their addiction.
- *You are free to explore the world and you know it's a safe place because you nurture yourself*, take care of yourself, respect yourself, and recognize what you need. In the same way, you extend compassion, warmth, and inspiration to others who are on a similar journey of self-discovery.

I find these qualities delightful and entirely worth the pursuit!

When you make this shift, those around you who are engaged in their Own Awesome Lives also shift. The "battle" you may be accustomed to – that of fighting to be heard – disappears.

You become able to build relationships based on reciprocal love, care, and respect.

Because you attract people who also have a strong
sense of self, no one is offended when you voice your truth,
and because you have a strong sense of yourself,
you are not offended when someone else
expresses their own truth

You and the people in your life are genuinely pleased that you are secure in your own convictions and are prepared to state them. And you're delighted when people voice their preferences, even when they're different from your own.

Conversations where thoughts, feelings, and perceptions are shared are treated with love, care, and respect. You don't hear, nor do you say: *"That's not really what you think, is it?"* and *"Why on earth would you think* that?"

Conversations matter. Others say to you, "Tell me how that feels to you," or "I can see you're sad," and you say the same things to others. This takes commitment because there will be people in your life who will see your efforts to reclaim your own Centered Self as threatening to them.

Your Self-Esteem is at Stake

Know that if you don't know your boundaries and don't know how to respect the boundaries of others, then your self-esteem is at stake. No, I'm not overstating this. **Your Centered Self stands on the foundation of your boundaries.** It's the most solid foundation stone you can put in place, for it holds and supports your decisions, your relationships, and your willingness to champion yourself.

Differentiation, as we have touched on previously, is your willingness to think, feel, and act separately from your tribe and to be okay with it – even joyful that you're being yourself. To differentiate yourself is to understand your boundaries and the boundaries of others. Healthy boundaries are your personal indicator that you are differentiating yourself.

I remember one of the first times I truly began to see myself as someone unique from my family. Although I didn't understand at the time the role that boundaries would play in this, I knew that feeling good about myself was not going to be found in being defined only by how well I thought, felt, and acted in accordance with my tribe.

It's worth considering:

1. Are you quietly resolved to live life according to your own blueprint? Or is the idea threatening, scary, or unfamiliar to you?
2. Do you explore, undertake, and complete projects, adventures, career paths, and decisions that differ from what your tribe would do? And are you comfortable within yourself when you do this? Or do you avoid that level of differentiation, or "rebel" and "defy" your tribe and feel miserable as you do it?
3. How do you feel about yourself? Do you like who you are? Do you believe in yourself? Do you enjoy your own company? Or do you doubt yourself?

It's best if you are as honest as you can with these questions. Just try them on and let them sit with you for a time. And then be okay with sitting with the feelings that arise. Please be compassionate with yourself as you do this. I bring this up because the pattern of telling yourself you're "bad" for not doing something is your old programming rearing its ugly head.

It's time to bring in the new! And the "new" is the same thoughtfulness, patience, and compassion that you would show a child when they are learning something new.

How You Learned You Were You

Your Centered Self – that wonderful, creative, spontaneous, playful, energetic, joyful you – needed to know she was her own person. Separate from her family. Distinctly herself. Wonderfully unique.

Not a mini version of someone else.

Not in comparison to someone else.

Not unique in a way that others had cultivated or insisted upon.

Your Centered Self, the unique You that is you, wanted to flourish based on *your own* thoughts, feelings, and perceptions.

Whatever you experienced, you considered it "normal" because it's all you knew. Now I'm going to invite you to step outside your tribe and see all of this as objectively as you can. You may recognize some of your tribe in the following descriptions or in a combination of them. Just know that loyalty to your tribe does not mean denying what was present in your tribe.

Your Centered Self is free when you see things as they really are.

Perhaps you were raised in a family that had **rigid boundaries**. If this was the case then there is little sharing of how people actually *felt*, and more focus on what people really *thought*. An example: When I was carjacked many years ago there was a "family meeting" to "discuss it". How I *felt* about a machete being held to my throat during the carjacking was not on the table for discussion.

In this family with rigid boundaries, logistics, how things appear to others, and fitting in by conforming (often enough by reinforcing "middle-class values") are the focus when decisions were made. Feelings and their expression are discouraged, frowned upon, or met with silence and stoicism. The members of your family would be disengaged with one another.

This family type is resistant to change and tries to maintain the status quo despite the need to change.

Ironically enough, the members of this family might describe themselves as being "close". It's true that they definitely help each other out with logistical tasks, like mowing lawns and fixing stuff. And yet typically the only person "allowed" to express strong feelings is one of the parents. The other Big Person is often mocked, dismissed or marginalized when she attempts to share her opinion.

That's a family with rigid boundaries. Perhaps you were raised instead in a family with **diffuse or chaotic boundaries**. In this environment, decisions are made based on *feelings, not facts*, even when facts would be helpful. Finances, for example, might be in disarray as purchases are made on impulse, and a lack of planning rule the day. "Sensible" conversations articulating differences of opinion rarely happen. Feelings dominate, with one Big Person's anxiety "triggering" anxious reactions in the rest of the family.

The high intensity of the emotionality means that children don't learn to think, feel, perceive and act for themselves. There is low adaptability to stress, and opinions which differ from the family ideology are perceived as a threat. Functionality is impacted by praise and criticism, rather than self-determined values.

This family is in crisis most of the time.

The members of this dysfunctional family may suffer from psychiatric disorders and issue threats of suicide to receive attention, which they settle for given the level of anxiety they had to absorb from the tribe when they were growing up. Each family member acts as if being individually unique is a betrayal of the family system. It's exhausting to be with them as their litany of slights, missteps, and outright lies become their attempt to hide their pain, but literally makes any and all attempts at conversation a minefield.

This enmeshment is a violation of the boundaries. Two or more people don't know how to operate as distinct individuals. Thoughts, feelings, and ideas must be shared, matched, and confirmed for everyone to feel okay. Intimacy becomes impossible given that no one is dealing with or communicating with a whole person… just fragments of who they are *supposed* to be.

Whichever of the above examples you identify with, if the boundaries were "messy" when you showed your unique self, you would have been judged, or mocked, or rejected, or suppressed, or in some way made to feel not okay as you. It may have been stated. Or it may have been implied, and you got the hint. This was the moment you learned to suppress that aspect of yourself. Your Centered Self, too fragile at this stage to fully express itself, hid from view because the price of revealing herself was too high.

You had to learn how to "be" around the Big People, so you never tuned into your Centered Self… the true You.

Your truest you – your Centered Self –
is in hiding and waiting for your invitation
to shine once more

What Happened?

Your boundary development stalled at the age when an event occurred that was traumatic, overwhelming, scary, or confusing for you.

Perhaps you can remember being abandoned, or threatened with abandonment. My father used to say, "I wish I could just go and join the navy and get away from you lot." I felt terrified that my protector would abandon me, so I behaved really well so he wouldn't. This was, I realized when I was older, an idle threat, but when I was seven it had power over me and stopped me from learning how to speak up for myself. I was too fearful he might leave.

You may have been neglected somehow. Perhaps you weren't comforted when you needed to be or reassured when you felt overwhelmed. You were isolated and alone when you needed a Big Person to wrap you in their arms and take care of whatever was scaring you.

You deserved to be comforted, reassured,
and often reminded how precious you were

If you were judged, belittled, or singled out, then your boundaries weren't respected. You were crying and sent away, or you were sad, and you were mocked. You may have done something that embarrassed you, and your Big People mocked you for it, and as a result, you felt outcast and alone.

Maybe your Big People's anxiety played out in their feeling threatened when you challenged them, defied them, or expressed a contrary view to theirs. Instead of being interested in your views and welcoming your independent thinking, they shut it down, got angry, and/or rejected you.

There were many ways your boundaries may not have developed:

- Your Big People expressed their insecurities by pushing their expectations onto you to be the "star," or be the "capable one".

- You experienced or witnessed some type of abuse.

- You had to take care of a Big Person instead of being cared for by one.

- People in your life demanded that you "act your age" when you were young, and you *were* acting your age. (They were really telling you that who you were wasn't okay.)

- If your feelings or thoughts were made out to be wrong… *I can't believe you said that!… You're being ridiculous!… I won't hear that type of talk in this house!… How dare you question me!?*

- If you were told how to feel and think about a religion before you had formed an opinion on your own. How can you develop your own views of the world if from a young age you've already been told what to think about it?

- As with religion, this holds true for sex, for gender identity, for sexual orientation, and for any version of sexual expression.

- Your Big People needed to be reassured or comforted, or they confided in you about something only adults should know.

- If you had to reassure your mother that you loved her, take care of her in any way, act as a go-between for your parents, provide advice, comfort, enable, or in any way deal with the problems your Big People had. In this scenario, you would have felt overwhelm, anxiety, and fear. You would have felt that your world was unstable and that it was all on you to hold everything together.

- You were smothered when trying to learn to be independent from your tribe. What you were meant to learn for yourself was smoothed over so you didn't learn how to handle the "bumps" of life.

- If one of your Big People was an addict, this meant you were secondary to the addiction. You had a relationship with the addiction, not with the Big Person. This was not okay. Yet you blamed yourself. *Perhaps if I was different*, you thought.

Other ways your boundaries may have been ignored, disregarded, or disrespected include being told to stop "wearing your heart on your sleeve"; or told to "man up," and "don't cry"; or you were punished without understanding why; or you were spoilt more than another sibling was, or less than another sibling was, and there were "favorites"; or you could never win your Big People's trust, no matter how hard you tried; or perhaps your Big People did not live a structured life, and everything was chaotic and disorganized; or you were not allowed a reasonable level of privacy.

The more this happened, the more enmeshed within the tribe you became; the more entangled and confused and messy things became and the less you knew who you were. Increasingly, you learned to align yourself with what your tribe preferred. Your own boundaries became indistinguishable from the tribe's anxious attempts for stability.

You hid your Centered Self and focused instead on where the next uncertain moment would be coming from. Or the next judgment. Or the next chaotic moment. Or the next feeling of shame because you didn't, somehow, measure up.

It Can't be *Them*...

Back Then, as a kid, I was so sure that *I* was the problem. If I could just be more... thoughtful? Studious? Praiseworthy? I jumped through so many psychological hoops as a child, trying to meet the magic standard of being "loved, adored, and accepted". I know my parents loved me, and still do. I also know they had insecurities that spilled onto us kids. It's also true that I don't see a parent who has it all together, so there's always going to be *some* spillage.

But I didn't know this as a child. Because "it" was my fault. Whatever was wrong, or going on, causing upset, making people tense... it was me; I was to blame. Here's an example: My parents bought a piece of land in the country. It had no water. It was my fault, in my child-mind, that I didn't know how to divine where the water was.

It *couldn't* be them. They were all-knowing! It had to be me. I was the problem.

Yet you're a child. Your very survival depended on them being able to protect you and provide a safe haven for you. You were as vulnerable as you were ever going to be... which meant that any flaws within the tribe couldn't include those of your Big People, because that would threaten your very survival.

The truth is that it would be natural for a child to take on responsibility to compensate for a lack of protection they feel. When your boundaries were not respected, or the boundaries of your Big People were put first and foremost at the expense of your own, this told you that you needed to change, not them.

It would never have occurred to you to have pointed out the way your boundaries were disrespected or ignored. You, as children do, accepted the way things were unfolding because, being a child, you didn't know any different.

Consequences

My internalization of messy boundaries meant I became a fabulous student, a thoughtful daughter, and someone who felt knots in their stomach whenever anything went wrong. Anxiety became my friend; my constant companion.

If there are echoes of this for you, then this is how feeling unsafe may have played itself out:

- You learned to stop taking emotional risks – you shut down vulnerability in yourself, and very likely in others around you.
- You learned to avoid making mistakes. The fear of being judged became so ingrained and conditioned that, if you're like many people, just the thought of not getting something right the first time was enough to prevent you from even trying.
- You didn't develop your Inner World, where you would expect to tap into determination and resilience.
- You never learned how to recognize your limits. You didn't know how to test them. You began to needlessly procrastinate, make excuses, blame external factors, or act like none of it mattered to you.
- If you were consistently denied your feelings, thoughts, and ideas, you began to lose touch with yourself. You began to lose touch with your future.

The more important the opinions of other people were, the less important your own became. How many times have you not trusted yourself? Doubted yourself? Felt anxious just at the thought of being judged? Felt self-conscious when you revealed some of your truth? Procrastinated? Held yourself back? Self-sabotaged? These are indicators of lack of self-trust. And they reveal how you have compromised You for others.

Your dreams don't die
but the persistence needed to achieve them
becomes an undeveloped muscle, and
withered with lack of use

The consequences of this are monumental.

You were denied the opportunity to stand alone with your ideas and bring them to life and full fruition.

You were so committed to the Big People,
you didn't learn how to commit fully to yourself

The highest price anyone pays when boundaries are not respected, nurtured, and encouraged is the loss of ability to go within for an answer you can trust.

You were hijacked.

Draw a line in the sand because *that stops now.*

Know Thyself

Isn't it time to move the focus from the External World to within you? Isn't it way overdue for you to learn what you prefer, what you believe, what you value, what you care about, what you enjoy, and what you love? Don't you feel the tug within you to discover and relish knowing what brings joy, contentment, and meaning to your life?

You will never discover the answers to any of these questions by letting others dictate this for you or by waiting for the answers to come magically to you.

You've probably already recognized that this will mean you will have to become intimate, comfortable with, and supportive of your own thoughts, feelings, and preferences. And that you will need to pay attention to and notice how you feel when you're alone – and how you feel when you're not. It will mean taking the time to reflect on how you're allowing yourself to be treated – by yourself and by others.

You're with You all day and all night, and you're the You you've got. Consider that the better you know yourself, the better you'll be able to recognize others who are able and willing to best mirror back to you the types of experiences you want to have. But this has to begin with you. No more excuses. No more delays. It's time to be the game changer of your own game.

Game Changer

"I'll do that when…"

"Maybe one day…"

"I'm gonna…"

How many ways did I have Back Then for avoiding… life? I wanted to feel awesome about myself, and to believe in myself, and to feel joy, and have My Awesome Life… I just wasn't prepared to pay any price for it. I certainly wasn't going to give up my bullshit.

What? Me? You're saying if I want these experiences I have to do something different?

Must be a mistake.

Then I realized that wherever my misery and disappointment was… there was I. It seemed the one common denominator was myself. Life wasn't delivering "Epic," but I wasn't exactly contributing from my end either. I was doing the least I could and expecting life to deliver roses.

One of the first choices I made on my road back to myself was to quit lying and quit making promises I wasn't going to keep. If I wanted life to deliver "Epic," perhaps I needed to chip in my little bit to tip the scales.

Game. Changer.

To respect yourself is to do what you promise yourself you'll do. When you lay in bed at night and promise yourself that "tomorrow will be different" and you'll start that exercise program, then you start it – or don't make the promise in the first place. (You can, however, lay in bed at night and say to yourself that you'd *like* to start exercising but don't know if you will.)

The internal conversation that destroys self-esteem is that in which you promise yourself you will (do something), and then you don't.

To respect yourself is to take yourself seriously when you make a commitment to yourself

To respect yourself is to say "no" when you mean "no". If you need to build up to this, start with, "I'd like to think about that and get back to you, thanks," if someone asks something of you that you're not comfortable with. Then go away and think about it, and decide if you want to do it or not. If you don't, rehearse in your head, saying, "Thank you for thinking of me, but unfortunately I'm going to need to decline this time." And then say that to whoever has asked the request. Don't justify. You don't have to come up with reasons. If they insist on knowing your reasons, then they're not respecting your boundaries. Just calmly reply, "As I said, I'm unavailable."

And don't keep talking. End of conversation.

To respect yourself means to be okay not trying to win over someone who doesn't seem to respect your thoughts, feelings, or preferences. They may talk over you. They may scoff at your ideas. They may judge you or try to shame you into changing your behavior. They may continuously let you down. They may blame you for their own emotional distance. Self-respect is to recognize these behaviors as not okay, notice how they "tension tag" you because of their own anxiety and indeterminant boundaries, and let it wash over you.

To respect yourself is to aim for less emotional reactivity over the same tired old arguments. It's to observe, not react. It's to think, not defend.

And you do this for yourself. Not for anyone else.

You, living Your Awesome Life, know you're on your own path.

Live Your Values

Values are what you care about, and they're revealed through what you prioritize. If until now you've prioritized whatever is the latest drama in your life, or habits that hold you back, or everyone except yourself, in the hopes of being accepted and liked, and you want to change this, you will need to change your values.

Your Centered Self can't flourish with this level of compromise and outward focus. Your joy and vitality cannot come to the fore as long as you live trying to second-guess others. If necessary, you will need to realign your values so that they allow you to explore who you really are, behind and beyond the habits you have that are driving you crazy. You won't necessarily get it right first time. That's okay. It's about exploring who you are with compassion and patience.

> *A values-based life includes values-based*
> *decisions, and values-based relationships.*
> *This means you drive your life in the direction*
> *of your dreams through conscious decision-making.*
> *You come off "automatic" and reactive living as often as*
> *possible and act upon the decisions that are*
> *aligned with who you're becoming.*

I was trapped in a cycle of emotional reactions to experiences, and unfortunately, the emotions experienced were "scared," "overwhelmed," and "rejected". There was no True North driving my thoughts or my behavior. Most days ended with me in a pile of self-doubt as I steadily traded my personal power for the chaos of blame and excuses.

When I considered the treadmill of overwhelm and self-pity I was on, it occurred to me that the one common element in all my experiences was, yet again... me. I then noticed that other people were having the same or similar experiences like mine, and yet they navigated these experiences without the drama I was generating.

At this point, it dawned on me that perhaps things didn't have to be this way.

As a result, I thought long and hard about what values and the ensuing character traits I was clearly prioritizing. I didn't rely on how I *felt*. Instead, I looked at the *facts* of my life. They were: ill health, loneliness, bitterness, hiding, avoiding responsibility, wanting to be rescued.

I clearly valued self-pity, isolation, and avoidance because that's what was showing up in my life.

Although I was saddened by my realization, I was also encouraged, for I had been able to figure out what I actually valued based on what I prioritized and experienced. Change my values, and I would change my priorities, which would change my experiences. And yet, I knew that living my new values would not be easy. My habits for self-pity were entrenched, and I seemed to be reluctant to release them.

I also knew if I was to have anything resembling My Awesome Life, I needed to change how I was approaching this. For my past neglect of My Awesome Self, I gave myself an "F," and I resolved to upgrade it to a "B-" over the next twelve months.

After much soul-searching about what type of life I truly would strive to experience, my new values became dynamic ones of:

Love
Compassion
Learning
Playfulness

And then I set about deciding how I would know I was living these values consistently. I made up some rules for myself about when I would know I was living these values, and I set the bar really *really* low so I could succeed.

Love…

I feel love *whenever* I think about someone I love. I feel love whenever I connect with someone, and we share a truthful, kind moment. I feel love whenever I spend time with myself and take care of myself.

Compassion…

I feel compassion *whenever* I make a mistake, recognize it, am kind to myself about it, and figure out how to navigate a better outcome next time. I feel compassion whenever I catch myself falling into old habits that allowed people to take advantage of me. Now I see how hurt I was and how I was trying to be accepted, and I recognize my energies are better placed living my truth.

Learning…

I am learning *whenever* I recognize an old pattern of behavior that was part of my conditioning, and I see how I am now making new choices. I am learning whenever I don't snap at someone I used to snap at. I am learning whenever I don't fault others for making mistakes, but show them kindness instead. I am learning when I show tolerance, compassion, and kindness to people who perhaps don't seem to like themselves or their world. I am learning whenever I smile at old conditioning that used to have me trapped, and I now see I am changing and making new, more empowered choices.

Playfulness…

I experience playfulness *whenever* I learn something new, try something new, and experience something new. I feel playful whenever I'm outside my comfort zone or notice that I'm overthinking something.

After I came up with these four values, I set about embodying them to the best of my ability, as much as I could. Initially, this process would best be described as a messy hit-and-miss. I was so conditioned to have my experiences shape me, rather than me shape my experiences. But there were moments… little moments… when I was playful. I felt loving. I learned. I felt compassion. Or I noticed these qualities in others.

This took conscious effort – true focus and commitment – when it was so much easier to slip back into old habits. And sometimes it took sheer bloody-mindedness. I had an advantage, though. I knew what "rock bottom" was and I didn't want to go there again.

As I worked my new program, very slowly my edges began to soften. The "brittleness" I was accustomed to feeling began to melt away. This didn't happen overnight. Nothing worthwhile ever does. But it happened with each new conscious decision I made and each new interaction I had.

You can choose any value for yourself. The key is not what you wish, but what you *live*.

To live the truth of values that empower you is to begin to know yourself and your Inner World

Your values could be about health and fitness and what you will and won't do to achieve vitality. I won't take prescription medication for my thyroid challenge, but I will see a naturopath and help myself that way. This is a personal preference that comes from how I value my health.

Live your values, regardless of the inconvenience, for the effort alone will invite your Centered Self back into your life

No one has to agree with your values or how you bring them to life. And that's really the point. These are personal values for you, and only you. They aren't chosen because others agree with them or approve of them. That would be pointless and defeat the purpose of the whole exercise. This is about you and your boundaries, and because of this, your values must come from you.

In addition to embodying your positive values – those things that give your life meaning – there are other ways you can establish self-esteem.

Make Self-Care a Priority

You might be amazed at the number of people I meet – men and women – who simply dismiss self-care out of hand. They don't have time. They have kids. They think it's selfish. They don't want to be judged. They'll do it later.

They are, without exception, closed down emotionally, stressed, anxious, busy judging themselves and pretty sure no one is noticing, so it's okay, right?

They're as hooked in their Tribal Cycles and the automatic living that comes with it as it gets. They're swimming in it. Drowning in it. But by God, don't question them about it!

Apparently, nurturing others is A-okay but nurturing ourselves is a ridiculous self-indulgence that only "weak" people do. Good to know.

Time and again in my conversations with them the pattern emerges of burnout wrapped up in a fixed smile, glazed eyes, and a weak statement to me that they're doing fine.

And it's a little chicken and egg. You need to think you're worth it to give yourself a little nurturing, and you need to provide yourself with a bit of nurturing to begin to feel you're worth it.

So you can turn down the chatter in your head for a moment, and accept that you're going to do some stuff that you've told yourself for years is pointless. And you're going to do it with care. And no matter how uncomfortable you feel and how much you just want to run off and get busy organizing someone or something or otherwise distract yourself, or act like you don't care, you're going to sit with what it feels like to pay attention to yourself.

Yup, sit back, strap in, and give yourself permission to put yourself first. When you start feeling like you're worth it, you can blame your coach.

Constant sacrifice for others may be the way you were taught that love is demonstrated. It's not. Love for others starts with self-love. We can't give what we don't see in ourselves.

Constant demands to be loved and validated by others may be the way you were taught love is demonstrated. It's not. Love by demand is not self-love.

Remember why you and I are on this quest. We're seeking the path to Your Awesome Life, to your Centered Self, and so that you can kinda dig You.

Start with – and let's go big, coz that's how we ride – honoring how you feel. Just feel what you feel, without brushing your feelings aside with a forced "I'm fine." Just stop that shit. And feel what you feel.

You may go further and express your feelings to someone who is capable of hearing them with respect and care. Acknowledge yourself when you do this.

Hiding wasn't working.

Now you're not hiding.

This is progress.

What about acknowledging your anxiety and your desire to be free from its grip? Or sitting in the sun and enjoying a cup of tea? Or going for a stroll?

How's your health? Do you exercise? Do you take the stairs instead of the elevator? Can you choose fruit over flour? Salad over sugar?

Back Then I lived in a perpetual state of it-will-be-better-when… So it was helpful for me to focus on learning to appreciate the moment, whatever the moment was, for *what* it was. My mind wanted to hijack my gratitude and turn it into *yes, but it could be so much better if…*

Given the misery this thought had given me over the years, and how many moments I'd managed to bypass, I persisted with this one until I could, with some consistency, feel appreciation for the here and now. And in saying this, I still have a long way to go.

> *Self-care is allowing yourself to appreciate*
> *the moment for what it is, instead of*
> *wishing it was something else*

There are many ways you can embrace and care for yourself. Perhaps what's available to you is to:

- Make decisions from your values, not the feeling of anxiety
- Not put yourself down to yourself or anyone else
- Say "no" to a request that's not aligned with your values
- Say "yes" to a new adventure that is aligned with your values
- Extend kindness to someone who is acting like they don't have much of it in their life
- Be less emotionally reactive to the anxiety in other people
- Acknowledge your own anxiety with compassion

- Be mindful, with quiet reflection, of your own enmeshment within your tribe
- Throw away outdated products
- Have a date night with your partner once a week or even once a month
- Keep your bedroom and your bathroom tidy, clear of clutter, with small touches that help you feel they're your sanctuaries
- Read a book that nurtures your Inner World
- Eat healthily when others would be more comfortable if you had that chocolate cake with the whipped cream
- Walk instead of driving
- Take the stairs instead of the elevator
- Hold back from judging yourself or criticizing yourself
- Learn a new skill
- Dance in your living room
- Turn off Facebook or any other social media platform for hours or days at a time
- Build relationships in the "real" world
- Learn to meditate
- Give yourself a break with a kind word to yourself when everything and everyone is crowding in on you, and it feels like you're going to implode
- Know when you're maxed and know you have to keep going and recognize you're some kind of champion right now for being able to summon the strength to do so
- Look at the full moon
- Wear your good underwear for no reason
- Use the "good" crockery just because
- Be less precious about control and more delighted with the spontaneity of the moment
- Acknowledge yourself when you keep going even though you feel overwhelmed, under-appreciated or taken for granted
- Speak up to say that you feel overwhelmed, under-appreciated, or taken for granted
- Watch kids learn
- Watch kids play
- Dance some more
- Let go, for just a moment, of how things are "supposed" to be

Or for you, it might be something else. For me, it's ensuring that each day I do something that moves me towards the life I want to lead. I love writing. It took me thirteen years of believing that I would one day be a writer to be able to give myself the time I wanted to invest in writing each day. I had to remind myself that it would happen, even when it looked like it was a complete pipe dream and I was only kidding myself.

Or self-care for you might be whatever helps you connect with yourself, and the version of You that you are becoming. It doesn't have to be anything grand or monumental.

Sometimes the moments that seem to be the most inconsequential can mean the most.

Be In Charge of Your Choices

This is your life. These decisions – to live your values and to care about yourself – are the vital missing pieces of your Centered Self. You can't shortcut this or agree that maintaining your values and practicing self-care are great ideas and then do nothing to act on them. The internal flame you have burns brightly because of your efforts to make your plan a reality, not in merely thinking about your plan.

No More Fixing People

Wow, do I relate to this one! Back Then I figured if I could put all my attention onto others, then somehow (I was unclear on the small print) my self-doubt would be magically transformed into empowerment. It was my version of "busy". It was my way of not having to deal with myself and what was going on for me. Focusing on "me" was hard. Make it about everyone else? Easy peasy.

This was also a form of control. Anyone I was trying to fix couldn't leave me. It was a gift for me when I began to have relationships with people who didn't expect me to be there for all their problems. This became even more delightful when I developed relationships with people who reciprocated the level of care and love I gave to them.

If you relate to this, I bet you're tired. And also, maybe you can see that this old pattern of behavior is really just a manipulation on your part to get love, attention, and/or validation. It's your way of seeking reassurance that you're okay. You will never be satisfied or feel fulfilled by this strategy because its focus is "Out There". You are not seeking to love and comfort yourself. This includes you trying to "fix" your kids. As a result, the void within will never be filled.

As long as your focus is on helping and fixing others, you are delaying your own restoration of your Centered Self. You are saying that their progress is more important than your own. You are putting your life on hold in an attempt to relieve the anxiety within you that you experience as you struggle to connect with others in a functional and loving way.

Start with not offering advice. I know. Deep breath. Just for a few weeks, hold back. Bite your tongue. Don't be "helpful". Be warm, supportive, and curious. When someone you care about is troubled, replace your advice with questions, such as:

What's going on for you?

What does that mean to you?

What's important to you with this?

How are you taking care of yourself right now?

Acknowledge their experience and assume their capacity to deal with whatever is going on for them:

- *That sounds challenging.*
- *You are capable of managing this.*
- *These moments are gifts to see ourselves more accurately.*
- *I don't have the answers for you. I respect this is your journey.*

And when someone asks you about you, tell them how you're really feeling.

Say What You Mean and Mean What You Say

Just to set the scene, I was feeling really frustrated and fed up. Someone I cared about called in the midst of all this. Yes, good point, I shouldn't have answered. Thank you. Anyway, I answered. They asked me how I was.

I told them how I was feeling.

They said, "Stop feeling frustrated."

I said, "No. This is how I feel."

They said, "Okay."

That, in my world, is what I call a major victory.

I didn't, as I was tempted to do, justify my feelings, bury them, "act" cheerful and hide behind lots of chatter about them, get angry when told to shut this shit down, get defensive, apologize for being a bother, or nag them about them trying to shut me down.

Like I said. Major victory.

I wish it were always like this. It's not. But it was a measure of improvement on my part. And I still struggle when someone bulldozes over me when I'm sharing a vulnerable moment.

But I do believe that a life can change in dramatic and beautiful ways from this one simple commitment to being honest about how you're feeling.

I've also noticed that when I communicate a boundary preference to someone and then stick to it, I have a much more peaceful, contented life. I feel free. I am free to be myself. I seek to be thoughtful about other people's feelings but not to the extent that I'll subvert my own self-worth in the process.

Be that person whose word means a lot,
and the people around you will spend a lot less time
taking advantage of you

I get it. This is not always received as a popular move. The people who are offended or upset with you for stating your position have their own weak boundaries and don't know how to handle someone who expresses their own preference. They're accustomed to you being a certain way. And now you're not.

"You've changed."

Yep.

Notice Who Is Attracted to You

One of the wonderful gifts of this new approach to yourself and your relationships is that the people who are attracted to you are also on their own journey of self-discovery. Centered people are drawn to centered people. Insecure people are not attracted to centered people; they're intimidated. And overly rigid people don't feel comfortable being around someone who is adaptable, open, warm, and self-assured.

Notice also that some people who were in your life now take more of a back seat. In part, this will be because you pull back from these relationships. And some of it will be because they're uncomfortable given that they can't make the same old assumptions about you anymore. The more you ground yourself in your boundaries and values, the more you will feel emotionally equipped to handle these relationship shifts.

Emotional Reactivity is Your Guide

Emotional reactivity is your guide as to how you're doing with this journey of reclamation. If you're still feeling emotionally "charged" when people in your life do "that thing they do" – which "triggers" you every time it happens – then you're still caught up in feeling, thinking, and perceiving according to the dictates of your tribe, rather than according to you.

Wow, this takes persistence. To get to a place where you can just observe, and be curious, and be open, and be uncritical when someone in your life does their crazy-stuff-that-really-pushes-your-buttons is tremendously freeing, and oh how I wish it were easier.

Your journey to restore your boundaries is for you. It's not to change *them*. It's not to "fix" anyone. It's not to make a point. It's not to win an argument. It's not to dominate or manipulate. You don't hand out lectures about how they "should" be. You don't announce how things are going to be different from now on. You don't "fix" anyone because you think it will help you feel less anxiety.

It's done so that you can restore your Centered Self.

It's done so that you can claim Your Awesome Life.

It's done so that you can reclaim You, which means letting go of your own emotional reactivity. This is the journey of a lifetime, and I know you're up for the job because, as you'll see and experience for yourself, the rewards are just too great to miss!

You're Ready

You're ready. You're ready to engage in the practices that give you your sense of yourself. The practices that guide you to self-love and self-acceptance. To a place where you know yourself, trust yourself, and value yourself enough to give yourself self-care, including letting people be close to you.

Now, we're going to move more deeply into your Truest Self, and acknowledge and embrace what is vital to you...

This Matters So Much: Ilsé Strauss' Story

Have you ever felt, *Wow, someone really* gets *me!*

That was how I felt when I first discovered Ultimate You through Sharon's training and her classes on social media. It was as though I was learning the language for what I was feeling, thinking, and dreaming of!

I was having challenges with my extended family at the time and experiencing a lot of shaming, mocking, and belittling because I wouldn't do or act the way they wanted me to. I wish I knew then what I know now…

Back then I believed that loyalty to my family equalled love, and that their pain was because I wasn't enough or didn't do enough, and as a result I had to conform to meet their needs. I believed I deserved the drama and toxicity because that was all I knew of "how family was done".

Yet after a lifetime of this toxicity, I was emotionally exhausted. I felt like my hurt was legitimate and should have meant something, but I was confused by what all of my never-ending emotions and reactions meant. All I knew was I didn't want to feel that sense of helplessness anymore.

And so the journey began…

I dived into Ultimate You. I discovered my Centered Self. I discovered my internal world. I discovered the magical thinking I'd grown up with. I discovered what it meant to take responsibility for me. I discovered that loyalty does not equal love, and I got to learn what love, care, nurturing, and compassion really look like…

And a whole new world opened up.

Personally, I have a much greater appreciation of my experiences now, and I'm able to create better experiences for myself and those I love. I have reciprocal relationships where vulnerability is valued, protected, nurtured, and cherished. There is a care and a depth of love with the people in my life – my husband, my children, my parents, my friendships – that I have never experienced before.

Professionally, I'm stepping up to a new level of success that I now know I deserve to have. As the fear of being judged, shamed, or belittled fades away, I know I can handle anything that comes along. And with this there's a new confidence, a new courage in me to build, create, and innovate the business I can see in my mind.

And already extraordinary things are happening! Just this week I received notice that my business has been named a finalist (for the category of "Innovation") in one of the longest running business awards here in Western Australia…

Meeeeee! A girl from the bush!

My journey to Ultimate You has meant the world to me. And every day it gets better. Every day I discover a little more about me. Every day I learn a little more about how to love. Every day I can give a little more to the world.

My life is more fulfilled than it's ever been…

Key Messages

- To have healthy boundaries is to have an invisible forcefield around you so you know what you're comfortable with and what's not okay. It means you attract people who also have a strong sense of themselves. You know that hell would be to be loved for someone you're not.
- Healthy boundaries start with you and require you to become aware of and develop the ability for active conscious involvement in your own Inner World.
- You blamed yourself if your boundaries were not respected and nourished when you were a child.
- If your boundaries weren't respected, you committed to the Big People and didn't learn how to commit to yourself. You shaped yourself into someone you weren't.
- You learned to protect yourself, prevent further hurt, and provide comfort for yourself.
- Your personal philosophy in life is limited to the extent that you had to sacrifice your own boundaries as a child.
- To restore your boundaries it's necessary to live your values, make self-care a priority, be in charge of your choices, stop fixing people, stop creating boundaries around others, say what you mean, and learn to tune into people who have healthy boundaries.

RESOURCES FOR YOUR JOURNEY

A companion worksheet, an exercise for you to do that relates to this section, a video from me, and more resources are available for you at:

www.ultimateyouquest.com/quest-support

CHAPTER 5

Your Fifth Gift:
Mindful Engagement

"At the root of every tantrum and power
struggle are unmet needs."

Marshall B. Rosenberg

Your fifth gift is elusive to so many because it demonstrates that you care about and respect yourself… and even love yourself… enough to become the adult you needed for yourself as a child.

A woman comes to me and shares that she's worried about her daughter. The daughter is struggling with… life. The daughter is angry. Verging on anorexic. There are many tears. School grades are dropping.

I understand why the daughter is struggling. She doesn't want to upset her mother by making demands on her. She has learned that her mother can't "handle it".

The daughter doesn't want to rock the tribal boat.

The daughter doesn't know where to turn.

So the daughter turns her frustration and hurt onto herself.

The woman wants me to coach the daughter.

<u>I want to coach the mother.</u>

The daughter is responding exactly as she should when a child is under pressure to "perform" for her mother and has no way of getting her needs met at the same time.

Each time we deceive ourselves and avoid the truth – the sometimes painful truth – about who we're being (clue: not our best selves), we create ripples of impact on our own lives and the lives of those around us.

"If someone is able to show me that what I think or do is not right, I will happily change, for I seek the truth, by which no one was ever truly harmed. Harmed is the person who continues in his self-deception and ignorance."

Jacob Needleman and John P. Piazza, *The Essential Marcus Aurelius*

You have needs – and when you neglect them, you create the lie that you don't matter. When you take care of your own needs, you open the door to your own self-worth.

Mindful Engagement

Mindful engagement is the beautiful gift of you engaging in life in a way that has meaning to you by meeting your needs. Your needs are the elements that are essential to you for survival, growth, contentment, and fulfillment. You, as for all of us, are driven to attain these needs, either through unconscious conditioning or through deliberate and conscious design.

When you learn how to, become capable of, are willing to, and relish meeting your own needs first and then the needs of those around you, you become centered and empowered.

- *You feel gratitude for the moment*, the experience and the opportunities that are both challenging and easy to handle, for they're all expressions of yourself and present you with the gift of growth.
- *You have stability without rigidity* so that the basics of life are taken care of, attended to, nurtured and maintained, including your core relationships, your health, your finances, your living space, and your career.
- *You have healthy boundaries in place for yourself and respect the boundaries of others.*
- You are in touch with, comfortable with, delighted by, and embrace how *you are uniquely you*, without apology or the need for explanation.
- *You are emotionally intimate with yourself and with your core relationships* to the extent that you and others are comfortable expressing your truth without apology, defensiveness, or aggression.
- *You know you matter* to yourself and to your core relationships.
- *You make progress* with yourself, which pleases you in terms of how you're growing and how you simultaneously feel content. Your life holds deep meaning for you.
- *You feel love without strings being attached or demands being made*; no manipulation is necessary.

To ensure that your own needs are met is to invite your Centered Self to take center stage of your life. In this, you feel the joy of knowing you can handle what arises with grace and groundedness. There is little to no drama attached to events and interactions, and there is much to be grateful for.

You, a Child

You and I, like every child everywhere, had needs that had to be met.

You needed to sense and trust that your Big People believed that you mattered, that you were appreciated, and that you were approved of simply for being yourself.

You needed affection and to be affirmed that you were lovable just as you were. And you needed accountability to give you a sense of responsibility and self-control. It gave you the ability to function successfully in life by knowing that the boundaries and rules that were in place helped you to develop and grow in a safe environment.

All of these needs were a vital part of how you would have felt cared for, loved, and safe. Any responses that were lacking, were inconsistent, or came with judgment attached came to be internalized by you as... *I am not enough... I am not worthy... I am not lovable...*

And then, there's enmeshment and your needs. When your tribe was too enmeshed, you became reliant on the cues, the expectations, the perceptions and the demands you grew up with. The high intensity of the tribe's version of togetherness may not have permitted you to grow to think, feel, and act for yourself. You learn to function in reaction to others. Because of this, the people in your family literally cling to each other for emotional support. The need for love is, in reality, the least emotional separation from your tribe.

You Tried to Help

Reflect back to when you were a child, to your "Back Then". You wouldn't have known to say "My needs aren't being met," or that you needed to differentiate yourself to free yourself of the addiction of enmeshment. Perhaps, though, you would have had a sense of it; of having to change somehow so that you could make things right for those around you.

You made "decisions" at a subconscious level, about how you "should" be and what you "should" do to be seen as okay and to be allowed to stay around and to survive in your family.

You unconsciously adapted to what you thought was needed of you. These adaptations can be beautiful aspects of yourself, or they can be self-sabotaging. Either way, they were a significant driver of the choices you made growing up.

*These adaptations became the visible manifestations of
what you had to suppress or deny in your childhood,
or what was a source of inner conflict for you,
and they have shaped your character in
impactful ways that determine
most aspects of your life*

Even if the character traits and habits you've developed hurt you or others, you most likely have come to depend, without even noticing it, on rationalizing, denying, and justifying to yourself the implications of your choices.

If you were encouraged to neglect your Inner World and to focus and concentrate on learning the rules your Big People wanted you to learn, then your skill is in how others want you to be and how to meet other people's expectations.

Again, this conditioning meant you arrived at adulthood ill-equipped to trust yourself.

You don't know that you can handle what may happen. When a stressful situation arises, you may be swamped with a feeling of dread and percolating anxiety instead of a feeling of personal certainty that you can handle it.

You don't feel mindful. You don't feel enlightened. You feel overwhelmed. Anxious. Uneasy.

Commit now to replacing these habits of a lifetime so you can live Your Awesome Life today.

Inevitable Unmanageability

My life looked soooo fine on the outside. My "coping" was to Band-Aid over whatever hurt, deny myself the truth of my sadness, and keep on moving no matter what. Never mind the out-of-control terror and the please-please-please-don't-leave-me fear of abandonment that was front and center in my emotional life.

You put defensive mechanisms in place because you were never shown how to get your needs met, or how to become uniquely You. You were never shown how to engage in life in a way that was meaningful to you or was mindful of who you really were.

Defense mechanisms are like circuit breakers. When an electrical system is overloaded, the circuit breaker is triggered, thereby stopping the dangerous surge of electricity from reaching its destination. **Defense mechanisms**

safeguard your mind against feelings, thoughts, perceptions, memories, ideas, or incidents that are perceived as threatening – that is, they are perceived as anxiety-provoking, and you don't trust yourself to be able to navigate them or navigate past them.

This unmanageability is the just-out-of-awareness anxiety triggered by your lack of ability to differentiate yourself from your tribe without feeling you're being abandoned. There are many ways this may show up for you today. You:

- Pretend to be someone you're not
- Hide your true feelings
- Suppress anger or sadness
- Procrastinate
- Self-medicate
- Self-sabotage
- Over-compensate by trying too hard
- Over-achieve
- Under-achieve
- Have dismal finances
- Be indifferent to your health
- Neglect your home environment
  (or manifest over-the-top perfection in your home)
- Be morally superior/inferior
- Experience constant overwhelm
- Display religious superiority
- Display spiritual superiority
- Exhibit rage frequently
- Are needy
- Are intolerant
- Are a people-pleaser
- Are always the expert and have all the answers
- Exhibit constant drama
- Are addicted to alcohol
- Are addicted to exercise
- Have a work addiction
- Are fixated on your finances
- Are fixated on individual men/women
- Have a drug addiction
- Have a gambling addiction
- Are addicted to sadness
- Are addicted to happiness

- Are obsessive about winning
- Are obsessive about power
- Are a perfectionist
- Are a control freak
- Sulk excessively
- Are determined to play the victim
- Repeat the same mistakes in relationships
- Are anxiety prone
- Constantly blame someone else for your own challenges
- Are addicted to sex
- Are filled with self-loathing
- Are engaged continuously in petty family squabbles
- Are addicted to social media
- Are addicted to TV
- Have a poor body image
- Exhibit emotional swings and extremes
- Have boundaries that are too rigid or too weak
- Have food-related disorders
- Have intimacy problems
- Have commitment problems
- Lie excessively
- Are a poor loser or avoid all competition
- Have a lack of genuine friends
- Are manipulative
- Are passive

Any one of these bullet list items provides an insight into how you learned to handle not having your needs met.

You adapted, and you did what you needed to do;
that part of you that wanted to protect yourself from
more hurt stepped in and developed "coping" strategies

It is the "Out There" or external substitute for the missing "in here" or inner peace you crave. It's far from the pathway to feeling that you belong, that you're enough, and that you can handle it. When you indulge your distractions, you're saying, "I'll delay dealing with me a little longer. That 'Inner World' stuff is hard. I don't know what to do. I don't trust myself to do it. In the meantime, I'll fake that I'm okay, or distract myself from my pain of not being enough."

Instead of looking inward and figuring out what to heal, you look outward to numb the pain of not knowing how to know that you matter.

Our journey together is to ensure that you give yourself what's been missing all along.

Your Needs – It's Time to "Adult"

To move towards mindful engagement in your life is to bring light, gentle attention to the choices you're making at the moment. It's to, with the softest of thoughts and feelings, notice a choice that may not serve you, and release that choice for a more centered one.

To do this, you must learn what your adult needs are, which allow you to:

- Heal yourself from not having your childhood needs met
- Differentiate yourself from your tribe to restore your sense of yourself and your self-worth
- Give yourself the guidance you need to help you know what is a mindful and centered choice for yourself

The answer is and has always been, within you

Let me pause and ask you, how many times have you read or heard that the answer is within and then thought… k… now what?

I did, for years. It *felt* true. Yes. *The answers are within me.* But damned if I knew where to look to find them.

So let's do this, step by step, so you know where to look, what to focus on, and how to meet your needs.

The question to answer is…
How do I be the adult for myself I needed when I was a child?

You already know you can't just keep doing what you've already done and expect things to resolve themselves. How many years have you spent dedicated to the strategy of the "child you"?

Waiting for "things" to change doesn't work either, does it?

Which leaves us with only one place left to look.

Within you.

It Stops with You

No matter how your needs were met, or not met, or met inconsistently, you're here now, in this moment, with the capacity to perpetuate the patterns in your tribe that have hurt you. Or to stop them.

I hold myself responsible to stop doing to myself and to others what I had been taught, which was hurtful or encouraged isolation and separation in me.

I decided that wherever I found myself feeling unworthy or unlovable was an opportunity for me to learn to change how my needs were met.

I recognized that my own neediness was my own addiction to love that would be relieved through me learning how to nurture myself and by discovering how to meet my own needs, rather than repeatedly turning to the patterns I had come to know through my tribe.

You need to make the same decision. The choice is firmly and 100 percent with you. No matter what you do, you can't feel okay about yourself until you release yourself from the neediness you feel. It's vital you learn how to meet your own needs. Doing this is the stepping stone to restoring your sense of yourself – to feel alive, rather than just getting by.

*There is a whole world within you that has been
neglected and denied for too long*

You feel this whole world beckon when you feel lonely or lost and (but you can't pinpoint why) afraid that life is passing you by, or when you find yourself distracting yourself from these feelings with the "busyness" of activities that don't fulfill you.

Together, we're going to restore your *Vital Needs*...

Make the commitment right now that you won't ignore yourself any more.

Tell Yourself Now What You Needed to Hear Back Then

You can't go back and undo what's happened. Your enmeshment when you were younger was inevitable. But now you *can* give yourself the gift of being there for yourself. Of learning to differentiate yourself by recognizing what you need. It's time to face what you've been avoiding and running from.

To feel is to heal

And to do this, you must face it.

Give yourself the validation you needed to receive. Start by giving yourself these four gifts:

- When you recall an experience from your past in which you didn't feel validated, or where the tribe was caught up in anxiety, give yourself the gift of saying to yourself: "I did not deserve that. I was a child. I deserved to feel loved, and that I was important, and that I mattered."

- Whatever – *whatever* – you feel as you recall a time (or the *feeling* of an event; you may not remember the event itself specifically) when you as a child were not comforted, validated, accepted for who you were, or in any other way denied your experience of you, **let yourself feel what you didn't get to feel when you were that child**. If you want to cry, cry. If you feel angry, feel angry. If you were disappointed but not allowed to show it... *Don't pull that face with me, young man!*... Let yourself, finally, now, feel that disappointment.

- When you're facing tough stuff, remind yourself that **you're a work in progress** and that the key is the *progress*. Tell yourself: "I am learning. I am willing to approach this in a way that shows compassion, patience, and calm. Whatever I did yesterday, today I choose to be a better version of me."

- When you face a situation in which you may be tempted to repeat a particular pattern of behavior that you know doesn't serve you, **shift into conscious awareness**: "This is me hiding from myself. I am choosing this behavior not because I'm weak or messed up, but because I have yet to learn how to meet my needs through my own Inner World. I am learning how to differentiate myself from my tribe."

Here's where the patience piece comes in.

Remind yourself that it's okay to feel hurt and that reflecting on a hurt is okay. Say to yourself: "I hear you, and it happened."

When you recall something painful or overwhelming from your childhood, let yourself hear the words: "You didn't deserve this."

In my own case, when I did this, I went on to let myself know that it wasn't okay, that I didn't ask for any of it, and that I deserved to be loved and protected, not shamed, embarrassed or used as the punchline to a joke.

A child is innocent. You didn't deserve it. Whatever you may think of yourself now, as a child you had no control over how you were treated.

Another way to communicate with yourself is to remind yourself that "It wasn't me."

No matter what happened – your dad was drinking, your mom was yelling, your parents were separating, your tribe was clinging to each other or shutting each other out, Big People were judging and shaming you, your needs weren't being met – whatever it was, it was not your fault. *No matter what.* Even if someone said it was. Even if you've convinced yourself it was. It wasn't. A child cannot be responsible for the Tribal Cycle they're born into.

You did all you could as a little child to be safe and to be loved and accepted; you did everything you could

You could have done no more. Your choices were decided by the Tribal Cycle, by the extent to which your Big People could handle their own anxiety without "tension tagging" you, and by how differentiated you became…

You were shaped by your childhood. You did all you could to accommodate what shaped you.

You did all you could.

Stop Blaming the Flower

Picture a garden filled with beautiful flowers. The garden needs, under the ground, good soil, water, and fertilizer. And above ground, the flower needs sunlight and the weeds to be removed so it can thrive. If any of this doesn't happen, the flowers will not reach their potential because the weeds will take over.

The garden's potential for beauty is reflected in how well it's tended. The question then becomes, "How are you tending to your garden?"

Perhaps you speak to yourself unkindly. Or you blame yourself. Or get dismayed with yourself. Or wish that your situation was different. Or that you were different…

If you didn't care for the garden, there would be little point in berating the plants for not flowering

You're the flower, and you're looking in the wrong place.

Turn your attention to what has been invisible until now. Your Centered Self flourishes when you learn mindful engagement…

Separate Loyalty and Love

One theme that recurs throughout my coaching with clients is the idea that to remember, discuss, acknowledge, or grieve the past hurts of childhood is somehow disloyal to the family.

I ask my clients to recognize that they can separate love and loyalty. You can love someone. You just don't have to be loyal to the family by keeping everything that hurt you secret.

A family is as wounded as its secrets

You're not "protecting" your Big People by hiding what hurt you as a child. You're only perpetuating the secrets for the next generation. You're going to hand the patterns of conditioning and hurt to *your* children.

It has to end somewhere. It can end with you.

Give yourself permission to recognize that you are separate and distinct from everyone else in your tribe. You are not someone else. Their "stuff" does not have to be your "stuff," nor should it be. Put the load down. Stop hiding the secrets and the shame that goes with them.

You deserve to come into the light. Defending what hurt you while you're still paying the price for it will only result in you inflicting more pain onto yourself.

Enough.

Two Worlds

See your world divided into two parts…

There's your Inner World – the stuff of your hopes, dreams, fears, values, beliefs, and thoughts. This is where your self-talk occurs; it houses your boundaries, your needs, your emotionality, your values, and your compassion toward yourself…

And then there's your Outer World, which is what the world reflects back to you about your hopes, dreams, fears, values, beliefs, and thoughts – and what you reflect out to the world: all that you believe is possible or impossible and all you attempt to do.

You experience your "Out There" (external) world based on what you project from your (internal) "Inner World"

Picture both worlds as the flip sides of a coin. They are both needed for the coin to exist and to be complete.

Most people are overly focused on their External World to the detriment of their Inner World. They worry about what people think, whether they'll be judged, how they're fitting in, what their family approves and disapproves of, what success looks like, and the size of their credit card bill. When they feel anxious, their focus on the External World tends to increase. They may turn to their addiction of choice. Or they may shut down emotionally or employ manipulative psychological tricks to feel relief from the tension. Or they may become super busy and stay externally distracted so that they don't have to feel their pain. They may blame others or attempt to control others.

Few people are taught how to focus on, develop, nurture, and fall in love with their Inner World

This occurs because, for many people, the Inner World is perceived to be a void, rather than the richly textured resource that it is.

Your Vital Needs

Learning to meet your Vital Needs provides the pathway to learning how to trust your Inner World – to be able to look within for answers.

This is how you learn that you matter and that you're worthwhile. These needs are the bridge to your mindful self – the part of you that is already alight with the truth of who you are.

Vital Needs are not optional. They are the very lifeblood of your self-esteem. To ignore these needs is to tell yourself that you don't matter.

There are four Inner World Vital Needs and four Outer World Vital Needs for you to learn to meet each and every day. By cultivating habits that meet these needs, you are teaching your mind to work for you instead of against you. You give yourself the gift of creating a garden rich with all it needs having been met so that your Centered Self can flourish.

Think of your mind as a flower. For it to be its beautiful best, it will need eight different nutrients. When any of these nutrients are neglected, the flower can't reach its full potential.

The Inner World Needs and the Outer World Needs work in harmony with each other.

Starting on the outer ring of what you need, are Gratitude and Stability. Then, as you move in through the rings to the center – your Centered Self – you come closer to knowing yourself, what matters to you, how you matter to the world, and what gives you meaning.

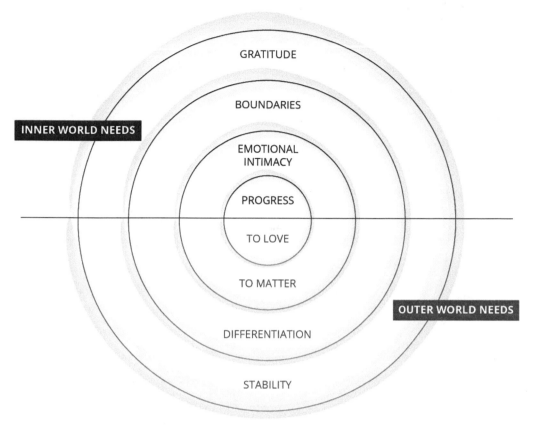

1. Inner World Needs –
   Gratitude → Boundaries → Emotional Intimacy →Progress

2. Outer World Needs –
   Stability → Differentiation → To Matter → To Love

The Inner and Outer World Needs are partners:

Gratitude/Stability

Boundaries/Differentiation

Emotional Intimacy/To Matter

Progress/To Love

As you learn to meet each pair of needs consistently, the next set of needs present themselves and become available to you.

Gratitude and Stability work hand in hand. The first is the internal need; the second is the external need. Having (internal) gratitude gives you (external) stability.

Next, we have Boundaries and Differentiation. Having firm boundaries (internal) allows you to differentiate your own individual self from that of your tribe (external). This is followed by Emotionality (or Emotional Intimacy) and To Matter. At the center is Progress and To Love.

Each pair of needs – an Inner World Need and an Outer World Need – work together to give you a centered approach to getting your needs met. When one need is met to the exclusion of the other, you'll be out of balance. You are not being truthful with yourself, or in some way you're denying yourself what you need. Any area of denial, suppression, or indifference you feel is a wonderful indicator to you of where you could become more mindful and attentive.

For example, you can't be emotionally unavailable to yourself or others and still expect to matter to others for who you are. You're not being yourself, you're not fully expressing yourself, and you're presenting only certain aspects of yourself to them. Others may not fully realize that you're not being your real, authentic self but *you* will know, and this tug of incongruity will prevent you from feeling genuinely connected to them.

Gratitude and Stability

Again, Gratitude and Stability are flip sides of the same coin.

Gratitude (Inner World Need) – Gratitude is the sun in the garden of your mind. If you consistently live this moment in preparation for *another* moment, or you're trapped in a distant moment or a distant promise of happiness, then you will feel perpetually dissatisfied with yourself and your life.

You need to know that this moment,
as it is, is enough

You can feel gratitude for this moment, for being alive, for caring about someone, for being loved, for being safe from war, for being able to think, for being able to feel the sun, for being able to eat without having to hunt for your food, for being able to learn. . .

Daily Practice:

- Decide in advance to be grateful for an experience or a conversation you will have today
- Express gratitude to someone for who they are
- Accept gratitude and appreciation from others

Stability (Outer World Need) – Stability is the soil you utilize and the weeding you do to help the garden of your mind be free to receive what it needs.

If you neglect your need for stability and structure, you place yourself under undue stress, which then distracts you from getting on with choices that can give you a more fulfilling life.

Think of stability as the foundation
of a beautiful garden

It's the planning of it. The organization of the materials. The seasonal planting. The regular, scheduled maintenance. It's what makes it possible to have the flourishing garden next season.

This fulfillment of your need for stability and structure can take the form of organizing your week, including making meals and doing the washing so that you have spare time during the week to exercise. It could take the form of planning your budget, so you live within your means as you save for your independent future. It could mean that you invest time, focus, and energy today into your health, rather than telling yourself you'll do it later. It could say, in a particular situation, be calm when you may have previously gotten flustered so that you're able to be a source of strength for yourself and those around you.

It could mean being the person others count on when there's uncertainty because you are the certainty.

Daily Practice:

- Be the source of calm and stillness when there's drama
- Don't *create* drama
- Have the simple things that you do each and every day organized in such a way, so you don't have to think about them

Boundaries and Differentiation

Boundaries and Differentiation are vital pieces of the same puzzle. You want to know that you belong in a healthy, functional way to your group – it could be your family of origin, your new family, a community, a club – and at the same time, you need to know that you have a level of individuality that separates you *from* the group.

Boundaries give you the
pathway to healthy belonging

It's through healthy boundaries that you know how close to allow people to get, based on their level of ability to love, care, and respect you and your preferences.

Differentiation gives you the pathway for healthy separation. It's by knowing how you differentiate yourself that you get to express yourself – both to yourself and to others freely.

Boundaries (Inner World Need) – Boundaries are the fences around the garden of your mind. They are robust enough to keep out what isn't welcome yet have enough of a gateway to let in those you trust. Some people can visit your garden. Some can stay. Some will never be welcome there.

Healthy boundaries include knowing what you prefer and don't prefer, what you feel is okay in relationships and what you feel is okay in your choices.

These are decisions you make for yourself about yourself, which then reflect onto your world. They are the healthy root system of your beautiful garden.

Each of us needs to develop our own blueprint of what our values are and to live this truth to feel a sense of self-worth.

With your healthy boundaries, and only with healthy boundaries, do you know where you belong, who you love, and who loves you. Anything less than this is compromise.

Daily Practice:

- Say "no" to something if it conflicts with something you have planned
- Express your preferences quietly and without fuss or drama
- Seek to understand the boundaries that the people in your life have

Differentiation (Outer World Need) – Differentiation is what you plant and how you have styled the garden of your mind to suit yourself, your preferences, and your desires.

You are valued for the unique individual you are

You need to be seen for who you are, not for who someone needs you or wants you to be. This beautiful garden has had its weeds cleared out. Here you get to flourish in the space that's been created for you, to be all of who you really are.

To be seen, validated, and accepted for your true, authentic self is a vital piece of your personal expression.

Daily Practice:

- Be okay that you're not the same as someone else, even if they want you to change
- Seek to understand and be open to learning how others see the world
- Ask yourself often: What do I want in this moment?

Emotional Intimacy and To Matter

Your Emotionality (Emotional Intimacy) and To Matter are partners on the same journey. You may have a very distant relationship with your emotions. Perhaps you struggle to label them, notice them, experience them, and embrace them. Or maybe you've already learned the importance of emotional intimacy, and you recognize, label, embrace, experience and then release your emotions with a deep appreciation because you've identified how they constitute a large part of who you really are. Or perhaps you are the type to deep dive into your emotions and live there.

In any event, your emotional landscape is a vital piece of your mindful engagement.

And we all want to know we matter. But we want to know that we matter for who we are, not for someone we're not.

Sadly, many people seek to feel significant in the eyes of others, yet they've neglected their emotional self. Their ego is in charge, rather than their Centered Self. The need for approval, praise, and acknowledgment can be its own form of addiction when your emotional world is not fully realized, claimed, and acknowledged.

Emotional Intimacy (Inner World Need) – Emotional Intimacy (emotional range) is you watering and tending the beautiful garden of your mind.

By owning, trusting, and being able to count on your ability
to experience, own, express and manage your emotions,
you can trust yourself to handle what is going to happen

Emotional Intimacy is the pathway to resilience, tenacity, and grit.

When you know you have access to your sadness, your anger, your joy, your happiness, you experience new moments without fear of being "found out".

Daily Practice:

- Acknowledge to yourself, with compassion, how you feel
- Let yourself laugh out loud
- Be present to someone else without overwhelming them with your views on their emotions

To Matter (Outer World Need) – To know you matter is the fertilizer of the garden of your mind. It's the source of encouragement; the boost you want to propel you onto new ways to embrace your Centered Self.

> *Everyone needs to be taken seriously; this*
> *includes by others and by ourselves*

If you continuously demonstrate self-care, compassion, and encouragement to yourself, you attract and are attractive to people who will take you seriously.

There is a part of you, and all of us, which craves and needs to be part of a broader collective. And you want to and need to feel connected and important to your group.

It's not enough to have a certain number of people in your life. You must know that, in their eyes, you are significant, and that you matter. That you are important to them. In your Centered Self garden, this is the fertilizer that nourishes you.

I'm sure you've had the experience where you've turned up at a dinner party and felt it wouldn't matter whether you were there or not. That the people there – and this could be your family – seem indifferent to you and your life.

And I trust you've had the experience where you've shown up at some other dinner party, and at least one person has shown an interest in and been delighted to hear about you and what you've been doing. You recognize that if you hadn't shown up, you would be missed – that your Centered Self is significant in their eyes, in their minds, and in their hearts.

You can also understand that you matter when you contribute to causes larger than yourself, the members of which are unknown to you personally or your circle of family, friends, and acquaintances, or though through kind acts to others who don't know you.

Daily Practice:

- Be with people who accept you for who you are
- Be kind to unkind people
- Contribute to something beyond your own life and that of your family

Progress and To Love

These two final needs, Progress and To Love, are how you know fulfillment. They are at the core of this journey to your Inner World. They're how you know you're on a path you care about. This is about giving of yourself without hesitation.

Again, one of these needs without the other will bring imbalance, which will cause you pain. I know too many people who believe they're "progressing" because they're reading lots of books on their "problem," yet they see no measurable improvement in how they love themselves or others.

Progress (Inner World Need) – Progress is the upkeep and the improvements you make to the garden of your mind because you know that to stagnate is to allow the habits of disillusion to creep back in.

When we wallow, we wither; progress is
essential for your Centered Self to flourish

When you obsess about something you don't like about yourself, without making a new choice or developing new and healthier habits, you poison your perception of yourself. If you become rigid and unyielding to the possibilities, you shut off compassion to yourself and others.

As we've explained before, rigidity is toxicity. To be stuck in your "comfort zone"… To be stuck in procrastination… To be stuck in a "rut"… These are all examples of a lack of commitment to your own progress.

If you relate to this, then the impact on your neurology is very real. You stagnate. You defend a status quo that doesn't fulfill you, and you reject moments that could be filled with beauty, love, happiness, spontaneity, and wonder.

A sense of progress… of growth… is vital for your self-esteem and for restoring your Centered Self. Again, it's the upkeep of your garden and this allows the garden to flourish.

To do this you must be willing to challenge your own mindset about what you believe, what you think matters, what you focus on, what you do, and the decisions you make.

Give up being right and surrender to the infinite possibilities ahead of you instead.

Daily Practice:

- Take one idea from this book and bring it to life today and every day
- Acknowledge where you have grown from yesterday
- Seek to explore new ideas that are contrary to or outside of your own experience

To Love (Outer World Need) – To Love means to tend daily to your garden… the foundation of the garden of your mind… it holds your future in its hands.

To Love is not about someone loving you – this is what boundaries and differentiation instill. To Love is about unconditional love for what is present right now, who is present right now, and how you are showing up…

Right Now.

It's the unconditional love that is
the point of the whole journey

This is the self-realization that it was always you who created your experience and it's you who is shaping this moment, right now. It's the love that is fulfillment, knowing that you're making progress and loving who you're becoming.

Daily Practice:

- Cultivate a feeling of surrender to the moment
- Love where you're at and fully immerse in this moment
- Be loving in this moment, and to who is here with you

Your Mindful Engagement Rests With You

There is, within you, a whisper that says you are worth it. That you are lovable. That you are enough. And that you can handle it.

This journey… to your Vital Needs… restores the truth that you are complete and that it's okay for you to embrace and express the you that is You without apology or self-consciousness.

This Matters So Much: Joe Pane's Story

Achieving what I thought was success I found myself under a cloud of emotional confusion.

My life lacked meaning.

I didn't have direction.

I wasn't enjoying my life.

And the thought of doing the same thing professionally for the next thirty years terrified me… Honestly, how could this be what "success" was cracked up to be?

In trying to answer this question, Sharon would say "The answer is, and has always been, within you."

What I love about Ultimate You is that, for the first time, I was actually shown where to look!

Through Ultimate You I have learned that the more I understand my Inner World, the better I am able to meet my own needs. As a result, my life has more meaning and I am more fulfilled than I have ever been before.

Sharon shares with us that our Inner World, where everything begins, starts with having a healthy gratitude for what we already have in our lives – whether that pertains to our health, our relationships, where we live, or the fact that we even exist at all. Gratitude contributes immensely to our sense of stability in the Outer World.

In becoming aware of my needs, the wisdom to know what to say yes to and what to say no to… I've learned that success, authentic success, comes from within. It entails taking care of both my Inner World and my Outer World, and its attainment has to be on my terms.

This brilliant Vital Needs model and the awareness that it brings to our needs, our internal journey, and our human experience is profound…

It's something I'm training future coaches in, for it has impacted my life in such an incredibly positive way that I want others to benefit from it too. As a result, it's now impacting the lives of my clients and their clients in ever expanding circles of conscious, meaningful living.

The language, framework, and models of Ultimate You have given me the gift of clarity… a clarity of how to think, how to be, and how to live the life of a professional human being.

Much gratitude.

Key Messages

- You, as all children do, had needs that had to be met. The extent that these needs were met reflects how well – or not – you are able to get your adult needs met today.
- As a child, you adapted and did what you needed to do. The part of you that wanted to protect yourself from hurt stepped in and developed "coping" strateges, which have manifested as the problems you have today.
- The question to answer is: "How do I, today, be the adult I needed when I was a child?"
- To heal yourself, tell yourself what you needed to hear, including: "I love you," or "This is messy and hard and I have no clue."
- What matters most on your journey is that you begin it.
- A family is as wounded as its secrets. You are not being less loving towards them by acknowledging the truth of whatever happened in your world when you were growing up.
- You have an Inner and Outer World. Most of us are taught how to attend to the Outer World but your Inner World is where you will find the truth of who you really are.
- You have eight Vital Needs: Gratitude and Stability; Boundaries and Differentiation; Emotional Intimacy and To Matter; Progress and To Love.
- To build your Inner World, do the eight daily practices to bring your Vital Needs to life.

RESOURCES FOR YOUR JOURNEY

A companion worksheet, an exercise for you to do that relates to this section, a video from me, and more resources are available for you at:

www.ultimateyouquest.com/quest-support

CHAPTER 6

Your Sixth Gift:
Emotional Intimacy

"Learning to infuse our emotional expression with compassion and discerning awareness asks much of us, but gives back even more, feeling and empowering our lives."

Robert Augustus Masters, Ph.D.

Your sixth gift – emotional intimacy – is so precious. It's the heart of who you are and cannot be denied.

To be alive is to feel, and the more intimate you are with your emotions, the more easily you can see the choices that you make with them. Emotional intimacy means you recognize, are comfortable with, label, experience, and understand your own emotions. It also means that you're able to be intimate, vulnerable, and open with others in a way that's meaningful for you both.

This isn't a simple thing.

You, like most people, have probably been conditioned to either distance yourself from your emotions and keep them tightly in check or to get lost in them and let yourself be carried away by them.

Being shown healthy emotions by your Big People would have been one of the greatest gifts you could have been given. I hope this was the case for you.

"Our emotions are ever-moving wonders, bringing together physiology, feeling, cognition, and conditioning, allowing us to connect and communicate in more ways than we can imagine. The more deeply we know our emotions, the deeper and more fulfilling our lives will be."

Robert Masters, Ph.D., *Emotional Intimacy*

What Is Emotional Intimacy?

Emotional intimacy is how you turn the key on the doorway to your Truest Self. Your Centered Self is emotional in the purest and most wonderful sense of the word. Your Centered Self is comfortable with feeling, without self-consciousness, or apology.

Your Centered Self is restored when your full range of emotions is accessible, owned, experienced, acknowledged, and validated.

Sadness. Anger. Happiness. Pride. Confusion. Uncertainty. Love. Puzzlement. Joy. Excitement. Melancholy. Impatience. Frustration. Compassion. Passion. Zeal. Enthusiasm. Humor. Playfulness. Irreverence. Disgust. Anticipation. Tenderness. Hurt. Disappointment. Warmth. Consolation. Affection. Anxiety. Patience. Surprise. Openness. Wonder. Contentment.

When you have emotional intimacy with yourself, you are courageous and undaunted when taking on new challenges. You're not intimidated by the thought of feeling defeated, or sad, or not in control.

- *You experience an emotion to its full completion.* You don't interrupt yourself or "reframe" yourself. For example, when you feel sad, you don't tell yourself, *"Spark up."* You don't dismiss your feelings. You feel what you authentically feel.

- *You're spontaneous.* There's laughter. Bursts of joy. Bursts of unexpected playfulness. There is a time for being stoic, but it isn't all the time. There is a time for playfulness, and it isn't when someone is sad or concerned.

- *You are present to and listen to others deeply*, without the conversation being about you.

- *No emotion you have or another has, causes defensiveness or hostility in you.*

- *You can be entirely vulnerable* and feel empowered.

- *You can empathize without a loss of your personal boundaries –* their story is not about you, and you don't hijack their story with your own emotions, needs, or need to share.

- *You don't ever feel as if you're a victim to your emotions* and you know they're not responsible for you or "making you" do anything. *You* are responsible.

- You know when you're replaying a pattern from your past conditioning, and you *can pull yourself out of reactive choices and into responsive, conscious choices.*

Emotional intimacy is you being available and comfortable with *all* of who you are. You feel no shame around feeling any of the "dark" emotions. All emotions are equal, valid, and necessary. Your Awesome Life is every shade and color of experience!

How Do You Get Along with Your Emotions?

Consider how it was when you were growing up, and where you're now at in terms of your emotions. How do you get along with your emotions, today?

When you grew up:

- Were any emotions banned or discouraged by your family?
- Was this different for different family members? Or consistent for everyone?
- Was one person, and no one else, allowed to get angry?
- Was one person, and no one else, allowed to set the tone for the day?

Now let's check in on your emotional life today:

- Which emotions do you access easily?
- Which emotions do you not access easily?
- Which emotions are people around you encouraged to experience?
- Which emotions are people around you discouraged from experiencing?
- What do you do when someone expresses an emotion you're not comfortable with?
- What do you believe the consequence is of not accessing all of your emotions?
- How often do you notice anxiety within you? What do you do with this feeling?

If you're conditioned to deny any emotions, struggle with the expression of emotions, or get embarrassed around emotion, you know you're conditioned to deny part of who you are.

And coupled with whatever emotions you deny yourself now are *experiences* you also deny yourself.

Emotions Denied

There was laughter in our family. There was fun. And when my parents were anxious, there was a rule... No sadness. No anger. No talking back. No defiance. *Don't be so sensitive... Don't you raise your voice to me... You have to stop wearing your heart on your sleeve...*

I was considered by everyone to be a well-behaved child. I never rebelled. I never skipped school. I rarely argued back. I rarely caused a "scene".

I complied, like a good girl. I shut down all "bad" feelings. I kept them to myself. I channeled my suppressed emotions into becoming successful.

My sister couldn't comply. She was, and is, naturally more emotional than I am. I buried my emotions in the face of perceived injustice whereas my sister's response to anxiety was to rebel.

Consider which of your emotions were possibly denied, suppressed, judged, mocked, or shamed by your tribe. You may have just picked up the "vibe" that "around here we don't express strong emotion," or perhaps you experienced the opposite, where it became about who was the loudest and the most dramatic.

When you were denied an emotion,
you were denied being accepted for yourself;
and you deserve to be accepted for who you are,
no matter what messages to the contrary you've heard

Toxicity Instead of Emotion

When a child spontaneously expresses an emotion, there is no conscious thought about it. Children, especially very young children, don't have access to cognitive reasoning. They feel. They express what they feel. This is how they communicate with their world, about their world, and about themselves in their world.

If expressing emotion was shamed...
If you were mocked, judged, rejected, or ignored when you
expressed a particular emotion, you internalize this to
mean that you are the problem

Whatever the emotion, it becomes attached to toxic shame. You may then exhibit that emotion less or distance yourself from it. Let's say sadness was not encouraged or welcomed when you were growing up. You came to link shame to the emotion of sadness, and now, instead of letting yourself access the emotion of sadness, you may instead cover it up with anger. You're sad, but sad is "bad," so you've conditioned yourself to express anger, a more acceptable emotion, instead.

You came to believe that you were the mistake but now,
as an adult, you realize that your child-self
was just trying to adapt

Swapping out of emotions in this way probably happened because:

- Spontaneous outbursts may have been discouraged, frowned upon, and rejected. Shame became associated with spontaneity and even to feeling the emotions privately. If this is you, you overthink things and procrastinate more than is healthy for you.

- Feeling deeply hurt may have been discouraged or mocked. You feel shame when you feel hurt, so instead of dealing with the hurt directly, you deal with hiding your shame. You may do this through bluster and over-confidence, by hoping no one tries to get too close, or by using humor or any other deflecting behavior.

- Anger may have been banned in your home so now, instead of feeling pure, appropriate anger when someone violates a boundary or deliberately hurts you, you may internalize your anger and turn it onto yourself with critical self-talk, or you may have explosive, disproportionate outrage in an attempt to feel in control of your shame.

- You may have been labeled "too sensitive" so instead of letting yourself feel what you feel, you try to bury the sensitivity in busyness, outward success, or other distracting habits so you don't have to deal directly with or acknowledge your sensitivity.

Toxic shame takes up residence when the emotions you were naturally meant to express are subverted. This subversion may have happened once or twice, inconsistently, or all the time. It may have been a dramatic moment of overwhelm and stress for you when a parent berated, shamed, mocked, or rejected you. It may have been a quiet reminder to change your ways. Or it may have been inferred through the behavior you saw in your siblings, which was either punished or rewarded. It may simply have been how you sensed you needed to be.

There Are No Negative Emotions

All emotions have their place within you, and all of your emotions are valid. To avoid some of them because they're too "negative" is to avoid aspects of yourself. Picture yourself as a ball, rolling through life. Now picture that ball being constructed of your boundaries, your needs, and your emotions. And now remove some emotions from the ball.

What happened? Did your ball deflate a little bit? Perhaps it started rolling in a wobbly fashion because part of it is now missing. Perhaps your ball stopped because the hole in its side is too big. This is the impact of denying a valid aspect of yourself.

If you label your more challenging emotions "negative" then you probably disproportionality value your "positive" emotions. This may manifest in behavior that involves being "super nice," or feeling bad when you don't feel as happy and upbeat as you think you should. It can show up when you feel guilty for feeling down, or hiding when you feel flat or deflated. It can show up in insisting people close to you "cheer up" and deny them their darker emotions. Or you look for the "sunny side" in an ongoing, exhausting demonstration of how "positive" you are.

Society seems to prize positivity and happiness. We struggle for it to be okay for us to express the full range of our emotions, whatever they may be. Again, however, by avoiding our more difficult emotions we only explore certain aspects of ourselves.

This can be a big mistake because it's by exploring these more difficult emotions that true healing may be found.

So let's begin today.

1. **Feel what you feel**. No distractions. No denial. No suppression.
2. **Label how you feel**. Be as clear as you can about what this emotion is.
3. **Own the emotion as yours**.
4. **Acknowledge how you feel**, without judgment or shame.
5. Allow yourself to **feel the feeling completely**, for as long as this takes. For example, if you need a good cry, go on and have it. **Complete the feeling and release it.**
6. Ask yourself **what you learned** and how you can grow from this experience.

Wherever your starting point… sadness… disappointment… annoyance… frustration… the goal here is to notice if it's been triggered by your own emotional reactivity and then recognize the cause of the emotion is not someone else or a situation, but your own automatic reactions.

Sit with how you feel. Acknowledge your emotional reactivity. You're human. These habits are ingrained over years of practice.

Feel what you feel, until the "heat" of it has faded. Then, if someone else is involved, express what may need to be expressed. Don't *react* from your own anxiety, or try to control them to relieve your anxiety. Instead, *respond* to the person calmly with what you need from them.

Train your mind to process the emotion, resolve to complete the emotion, then move to "frame" the emotion and the experience that led to it in such a way that it becomes possible to turn it into something valuable for growth, for fulfillment, for self-worth, and for love.

Feelings Aren't Facts

As you think your thoughts, your neurology fires off sequences throughout your brain that produce specific chemicals to match those thoughts for you to be able to feel the way you think.

When you focus on joyous thoughts, chemicals that match these thoughts are released throughout your body.

When you focus on depressing thoughts, the same thing happens.

What you become familiar with and practiced at creates a neurological network that, over time, becomes entrenched. When this happens, opposing thoughts and feelings aren't as easy to access.

The danger is when you allow your feelings to become your thoughts, and think that they're facts.

Dr. Joe Dispenza shares in *Breaking the Habit of Being Yourself*: "When feelings become the means of thinking, or if we cannot think greater than how we feel, we can never change. To change is to think greater than we feel. To change is to act greater than the familiar feelings of the memorized self."

Reclaim your brain:

- Feelings aren't facts.
- No one else has to feel what you feel.
- You don't have to feel what someone else feels.
- You can train your brain to think its way through your feelings.
- Anxiety in the face of new situations, relationships, and commitments is opportunity for growth, as it's a clue to your own lack of meeting your needs to achieve differentiation.

Pause the next time you're in the whirlwind of emotion, which you "think" is all there is. Just. Pause. Five. Four. Three. Two. One.

Now ask yourself any or all of the following questions:

- Am I responding accurately to this moment, or am I reacting to my own anxiety?
- Once this experience is complete, which values will I have expressed?
- It's twelve months from now... Was this worth the storm?

Feelings are not facts. They cannot become your controlling force. They have a place, as do your thoughts. Allow yourself the space to see that clarity is within you.

Vulnerable You

Being emotionally vulnerable is a courageous and daring act of reclaiming yourself. It's a declaration of determination to be who you truly are, without denial or apology. Sharing a vulnerable truth with another is transformative and boosts your self-esteem. When you do this, you in effect declare that you are willing to risk possible rejection because you know you matter.

Vulnerability requires you to be honest with yourself

Vulnerability requires honesty about which emotions you've been denying yourself or how you've twisted one emotion into another – such as sadness into anger. It requires calling yourself out about how you may have manipulated others, so you don't have to feel what you feel, or so that they don't perceive you as being vulnerable. It requires facing how you've been defensive, aggressive, or dismissive in moments that have called for genuine and heartfelt emotional truth.

To be emotionally intimate is not a secret job undertaken when no one is looking. Emotional intimacy calls for the act of vulnerability to be witnessed and validated by another.

There is something wonderfully freeing and healing about allowing another person to see a genuinely vulnerable moment in you, and have it treated with the tenderness and respect it deserves.

You're an adult, now.

You're no longer a child.

You have power to choose someone who will see you for the courageous seeker of truth that you really are

Emotional honesty requires you to speak up about when you're hiding, denying, or being incongruent with how you feel. It may be scary to drop your guard because you're used to feeling afraid of this. But to stay hidden is to turn away from your Centered Self – from the true essence of who you really are. You are, no matter how much you may wish to deny it, an emotional being.

Here are some ways that you may further explore this for yourself:

1. Tell someone you trust how you really feel. "I feel sad," "I could do with a hug," "I'm not sure how to approach this."
2. If someone you trust shuts you down, point it out: "Hey, I was sharing something important. I'd like to be heard."
3. Let people close to you share how they feel, and don't interrupt them, try to solve anything, offer advice, or tell them they're over-reacting.
4. Recognize the emotional reactivity in others. Don't react with your own emotionality. Respond with compassion. With clear boundaries. With the refusal to perpetuate the dance of enmeshment.

To connect with yourself and with others is going to take self-revealing honesty – anything less is to remain marooned in your past. Is that where you really want to be?

Compassionate You

To be willing to develop this relationship with yourself takes more than courage. It also takes compassion. When you decide to face how you feel, with all its rawness, weirdness, discomfort, and/or shame, you're declaring that your internal world is a compassionate zone. You alone can give yourself this gift.

Compassion doesn't involve self-pity, or feeling like a victim, or deciding to give up because it's too hard, or experiencing a feeling of defeat. Those things constitute toxic shame, making you want to hide, run, and deny anything that even remotely feels like it might be a profound moment full of meaning.

Compassion is your willingness to do what you need to do to heal yourself from your past. It's the moment when you interrupt the gremlin in your head that is spewing criticism and saying *Hang on… that's enough… I don't deserve that.*

> *Compassion is you seeking, with dogged persistence,*
> *the Inner World within you that provides you*
> *with guidance, wisdom, and certainty*

This is the compassion that comes from knowing Your Awesome Life awaits you. Bring your compassion to life in the following ways:

- Speak compassionately to yourself.
- Pause before you criticize – is your snarky comment really going to improve anything?

- Share a kind word when someone makes a mistake instead of judging them.
- Seek to understand someone rather than to be understood.
- Be fully present to someone, without it being about you.
- Let someone be fully present to you, and honor this moment with truth.
- Make a mistake, and recognize, with practice, that it doesn't mean that *you* are a mistake.
- Be compassionate and calm in the face of emotional reactivity.

Compassion can mean letting the moment unfold without you judging yourself.

Take Responsibility for Your Emotions

Emotions don't "happen" to you. They are a part of you. They are conditioning. They are what you practice. They're what you have trained your mind and body to feel.

When you were a baby, you felt what you felt. Any and all of it. Without thought. Without filters. Without self-consciousness.

Then you noticed, because your life depended on it, how the Big People responded to you. And you adapted. To fit in. To survive. To get approval. To gain acceptance. To not be rejected or abandoned or shamed.

And that became your emotional range.

But it's not.

Today you are more than what you were taught as a child. You're an adult. You can't still say it's the "Big People".

This is especially true if you're people-pleasing and overly sensitive to other people and their emotions. You will subjugate your emotions for other people. Again, as in childhood, you place yourself last in terms of emotional care.

There are other ways that you can't process how you feel in a centered and healthy way. You give someone the "silent" treatment. You storm off. You hold a grudge. You blame the other person for "making me" feel this way, instead of taking responsibility for your emotions. You feel the anxiety of your own emotional reactivity and blame someone else or the situation.

None of this will move you toward restoring your Centered Self. It could never do this because there is no compassion here.

It's now time to own your emotions;
to take responsibility for how you feel

It's time to stop blaming anyone else for how you feel. It's time to stop justifying repeatedly staying stuck in the emotions that hinder your Centered Self. It's time to allow yourself the gift of emotional intimacy.

Ways to Avoid How You Feel

There are so many creative ways by which we bypass our emotions. This is not deliberate, however, and most of us aren't even aware that we do it. The distractions are defense strategies that can become aggressive strategies to avoid dealing with the emotion.

Consider honestly the diversions you've adopted to avoid dealing with how you actually feel:

- Turning the emotion that makes you feel vulnerable or uncomfortable into another, more "powerful" emotion such as anger or hostility.
- Ignoring the emotion.
- Finding busy things to do so you don't have to focus on the feeling.
- In moments that could become personal or "too close" to home, you change the subject.
- In moments that could become personal, you say something inflammatory to upset the other person, so now the conversation is about something else.
- You keep the subject on logistics, on activities, and concepts: "safe" topics.
- You say, "I don't know," when you're asked to express an emotion.
- You say, "What does it matter?" when someone close wants to explore a personal topic.
- You shrug and retreat.
- You blame the other person for "always making things complicated".
- You act puzzled like the other person is nuts or way off base.
- You declare you're too tired to talk about this now, and you're always too tired/busy/occupied to talk about it.
- You never initiate conversations about how you feel.
- You never admit to how you feel if you link shame to the feeling.

- You deny there's a problem and declare the other person is "making too much of a fuss".
- You think activities like watching TV are "intimate".
- You use humor to distract and run camouflage on how you feel.
- You remain stoic and "together" during stressful discussions as if being "together" shows you're the reasonable person in the discussion.
- You act "cool" and unflappable.
- You mock the qualities of sensitivity, vulnerability, and compassion.
- You disregard someone's emotions and act like nothing is amiss.
- You are dissociated from how you feel: numb and disconnected.

This list isn't complete, I'm sure. You may have your own unique ways of avoiding the emotion. And I know I've said this before, but it bears repeating… much of this is unconscious and runs on automatic pilot.

And yet, you can change it.

All of it.

Start with These Seven Emotions

I felt all of these seven emotions regularly Back Then, but I would have denied it by arguing with you about it. I would have told you I'm all good. Anything but face my emotions too closely.

Fear. Anger. Happiness. Disgust. Surprise. Sadness. Anticipation.

And then… **toxic shame**.

These initial seven emotions can be considered the primary or core emotions from which most other emotions spring. They existed long before you had conscious thought, or utilized language, or could even understand what you felt.

You simply… felt.

Let's give ourselves some quiet time to sit and reflect on how we feel. Just notice. Nothing else. Let yourself be with how you feel. This may seem unfamiliar, uncomfortable, confronting, scary, pointless.

Do it anyway.

Simply notice what and how you feel. If it's a challenge for you to know or identify what you feel, use the above list to guide you, and try each of the emotions on. Do you feel fear? If so, notice and acknowledge it. Don't run from it or shut it down. Let it be with you. This is the beginning of emotional intimacy with yourself.

Right now, as I write these words, I feel sadness. I've just had an experience in which I felt let down and disregarded. Between typing, I'm sitting with how I feel, honoring how I feel. It's okay to feel what I feel. I don't have to snap out of it. Or "Spark up." I wish I didn't feel sad. But I do. And I'm not rushing to get "happy" because that's what "positive people" do. I'll get there. Happiness is an emotion I sit with, too.

Just not in this moment.

Then there's the eighth emotion... The hostage-taker of all your other emotions... Toxic Shame. Shame says you feel bad because of an action. Toxic shame says you feel *you* are bad.

Maybe, as you sit with how you feel, you notice how you feel about how you feel... If you feel "happy," how do you feel about feeling happy? There's a whole conversation to be had about who you're observing. Yourself? Your mind? And if so, who's observing your mind? Yourself? Sorry, I went esoteric on you there for a moment; I'm back now. (But isn't it fascinating?)

Any of the above seven emotions may be laced with the poison of toxic shame. To even feel the emotion may cause you to feel shame, and so you shrink away from it, avoid it, deny it, dismiss it as "over-reacting" or pretend it's just not happening.

Any of these reactions are an avoidance of the emotional intimacy that is crucial to you and to your personal relationships.

How you relate to yourself and to others
is determined by the emotional access you have and allow others
to have, without defensiveness or aggression

If you notice yourself doing any of the distracting strategies listed earlier:

- Acknowledge that you've noticed what you've done.
- Acknowledge that it's not helpful.
- Return to the emotion.

If you're with someone you trust, turn toward your emotional disconnection with honesty and compassion. It's not who you are, it's a strategy you learned. You're facing it, dealing with it, and changing it. Recognize that there is no true escape from feeling, no matter how painful the feeling may be. The emotion is there; it's just being played out in unhealthy and unhelpful ways. So turn toward it in a way that you would have wanted to be faced when you hurt as a child. Bring your compassion and patience and openness to the situation.

You may feel shame as you feel the emotion. You may feel shame because you recognize you've been so out of touch with yourself for so long. You may feel shame because you realize you're emotionally absent from close relationships. This is normal. Let the feeling float *through* you, or it will become your focus.

If you're unsure how to label what you feel, just get a sense of it and pay attention to your bodily sensations. You may (or may not) feel tightness in your chest, in your gut, or in your neck. You may feel uncomfortable and restless.

Whatever is happening, let it. You may find a strong desire to use one of your distraction techniques. That's okay. If it kicks in, notice it, acknowledge yourself for noticing it, and then go back to the emotion.

Dr. Russ Harris, in his book *The Happiness Trap*, shares: "Why develop willingness? Because throughout your life uncomfortable feelings will arise. If you keep trying to avoid them, you'll simply create additional 'dirty discomfort.' By making room for your feelings and willingly feeling them (even though you don't want to), you'll change your relationship with them, they'll become much less threatening and will have less influence on you."

This is the first step towards your emotional intimacy. It's a slow dance. It's not a sprint.

Keep dancing. Because you're worth it.

Practice Being Present to the Emotion

The other day I had what I consider an awful experience with a medical professional. She mocked my efforts to engage in a real discussion about my health, dismissed my hurt feelings as my problem, and told me if I was offended I was too sensitive. I shared, after she'd made several assumptions about my health, that she didn't know me. She responded by saying I didn't know her either. I said that's not really the point, as I'm the patient and I'm sure I don't need to get to know her health issues. She rolled her eyes at me. I respectfully asked that she stop making jokes at my expense, which was ignored. I was crestfallen because I'd pinned my hopes on the outcome of this appointment, anticipating that it would give me answers I'd been seeking for quite a while. I cut the appointment short and told her that I wasn't comfortable with her or her manner, and left.

In the past I would have been "stoic," made light of it, not said a word to anyone in case they saw my vulnerability and dismissed the unease I was feeling.

This time, I cried.

I felt sad that this appointment had been such a horrible experience. I noticed I felt humiliated that my health concerns had been dismissed and mocked. I felt angry that someone could behave so unprofessionally. I felt disappointed and deflated that a two-month waiting period for an appointment had ended up being a total waste of time.

I also felt proud with myself for expressing my needs to her so clearly, even though they were ignored. I felt pleased I'd respected my own boundaries and had gotten out of there. And I adored how I didn't appear to have it all "together" for the sake of being perceived as "strong" by the people in my life.

I let myself really feel what I was feeling, noticed the emotions, sat with them, didn't rush them, didn't dismiss them, acknowledged them fully, embraced them, and then got on the phone with people who validated me beautifully until I could laugh about it.

Throughout this experience, I deliberately took the steps I knew I needed to take to move through this upsetting event. For me, this was not a quick journey to this moment. It took me years to overcome decades of entrenched "coping" – a result of my having suppressed my feelings over such a long period.

Give yourself the gift of being present to your emotions

There's no rush with this. You may be dissociated from your emotions and not connect with them in the beginning, particularly if you experienced trauma as a child, including any form of abuse. This is a normal occurrence as your child-you kept you safe from feeling the emotions you were too young to experience.

Again, simply stay with this. Emotional intimacy, like physical intimacy, is not to be rushed. Take your time just sitting with how you feel. Be present to yourself as you wished you had been as a child.

Share with Someone

By giving your feelings a voice, you are reclaiming aspects of You. No drama, please. Just you, stating what's going on for you in the moment. Share this with someone you trust and who you've briefed on the situation so that they know you need their focus and attention.

Ensure you share what you feel, rather than describe what happened. Often someone who's new to this will share something like: "My tummy feels tight." This isn't a feeling, it's a description of how their body is responding to the feeling.

Use one or more of the core emotions – fear, anger, happiness, disgust, surprise, sadness, anticipation – in your sentence, to ensure you're learning to voice your feelings.

You may notice that you experience some shame when sharing your feelings. This is normal for you in that no doubt you felt shame in the same scenario when you were a child. Share this too. Keep it simple. "I feel shame as I share this."

Resist the backstory, the need to explain yourself, the need to justify why you feel this way, or blaming any other person as being at fault.

This is merely being present to your feelings with someone being present to you; the gift of this emotional intimacy is you will both feel closer and more deeply connected

Learn the Language of Emotion

There is a language of emotion that you can learn to access if you can't already. If that's the case, skip this exercise. If you've learned to shut down some emotions or avoid talking about them, then this is for you.

Remember: You're worth it.

As part of you taking responsibility for your emotions, learn the language of emotion.

If you do have a limited or narrow range of emotions you tap into, you will also have a narrow range of language to indicate your emotions.

It's time to expand your vocabulary around emotions.

Start listening intently when someone shares their feelings. What language do they use to express themselves?

Start reading books and articles that bring out some of these formerly taboo emotions within you. Typically these are where your emotional blind spots are.

If you're unfamiliar with "happiness," learn how to language this.

If you're unfamiliar with "sadness," learn how to language this.

Whatever has been unavailable or mysterious to you, decode with language

For example, when it comes to the language of sadness…

I'm feeling out of sorts…

I'm upset…

I don't feel right…

I feel sad…

I'm bummed out…

You're not the only person who has emotions, who struggles with emotions, and who wants to express their emotions. Every single person you meet or speak with or think about is also having feelings, is wanting to express feelings, is wanting to bottle up feelings…

To be human *is to feel*.

Each time you're with someone, and there is a conversation about feelings, pay attention. Be emotionally supportive.

You ask, "How are you?"

They answer, "I'm fine."

Notice how they look. Do their demeanor and expression match their words?

If you see they're a little slumped, can't make eye contact, seem distracted, or just seem "off," ask about it…

"Tell me. What's going on?"

They may share. They may not.

Stay engaged. Maintain eye contact. Look neutral. Be open to whatever may be going on for them.

They say, "I guess I'm feeling a little overwhelmed at the moment."

You say, "How come?"

They say, "It's work. So much to do."

You say, "Tell me more…"

They say, "It's a deadline I missed. I'm disappointed with myself."

You say, "It matters to you…"

They say, "Yes. It does."

You say, "Hmmm… I appreciate its importance to you. I'm here for you."

No reframing. No advice. No lectures. No solutions. No "Spark up" speeches. No changing the subject.

Just be with them, fully.

Don't expect anything in return.

Just do it, for them.

You Are Equal

An audience member doesn't want to take up my time. Our time. She's apologetic for the time she's taking, which could be spent on "getting on with it," and on "helping other people."

She's so accustomed to being invisible that she doesn't know how to accept that it's okay to be first.

The conversation we were going to have becomes about her being okay with being first on everyone's list.

It's uncomfortable for her.

She apologizes again. And when I show I clearly don't need the apology, and nor do the audience members, she gets angry.

She's really afraid. But she masks it with anger. "I don't want to discuss this, anymore."

Which is her right. Of course.

But it's obvious this isn't about her not wanting to discuss it. It's about her not knowing how to recognize when it's her time to discuss what is going on with her.

How you feel is how you feel. No one's emotions are more important, or take priority, over anyone else's. You are not required to bury your emotions, or ignore your emotions, or deny how you feel to give priority to someone else's emotions.

Don't let anyone's emotions be more
important than your own

You're in an intense discussion with your partner. They feel agitated and frustrated by you not doing what they want you to do. You feel upset about compromising, again. Feel agitated. Goodness, feel how you feel!

No apologies needed.

No justifications required.

Just feel what you feel.

You can agree to disagree.

What you *can't* do, when recovering your emotional range, is to bury yet again how you feel, and so allow someone else's feelings to possibly eclipse your own.

You can say, "I feel strongly about this. I'm not changing my mind. I realize we see things differently. That's okay with me. Let's agree to disagree."

You can say, "It's okay for me to be mad about this. That's the third time this month you've let me down. You said you'd do it. You didn't do it. And now you're making excuses instead of taking responsibility for not showing up. I'm okay feeling upset about this. You can't control how I feel about this with your excuses."

Yup. It's okay to say that.

You can say, "I feel pleased with what I've done. I realize you're not happy with me. That's a sad thing. But it's not going to detract from my happiness. I did good. I love what I did. I'm proud of myself. And I feel great about it."

You can say, "Yelling at me isn't going to make me feel bad. I am having a great day. I have a lot to do today. You want attention. I get that. And later, when I've done what needs to be done, we can spend some time together. Or you can help me with what has to be done around the house. But whatever you decide, I'm in a great place. I'm focused, and I'm determined to get things done."

You can say, "Hey, don't rain on my parade. I shared something that makes me happy. You don't get to bring me down."

You can say, "I love how you are happy for me like I'm happy for me. I appreciate that you're with me on this. It means a lot to me. I love it when we get to share great times together."

You can say, "Thank you for seeing my sadness. I feel loved when you see me for how I genuinely am."

These are, clearly, simply some examples of how to respond. They are unlikely to be exact word-for-word phrases that you can use. The patterns of how to address emotional imbalance are there for you.

No Hostages

What your journey to your Centered Self means is to embrace all of you, even the bits you have previously ignored or neglected or denied are there.

It's confronting. Sometimes complex and muddled.

And sometimes, you will be tempted to justify "making" someone else the recipient of all your baggage, drama and reactivity. You will, in effect, take them "hostage".

This is not moving you towards your Centered Self. It's the neediness you feel being fully indulged. It won't move you anywhere but towards more emotional reactivity.

Know that this quest is *not* to keep looping into your own emotional reactivity; nor is it about "getting it all off your chest". It's recognition of your anxiety. It's compassion for yourself as you don't indulge the desire to dump your anxiety onto someone else. It's to see yourself accurately. It's responding to the situation before you, free of the emotional reactivity that has held you hostage for too long.

Persist. Practice. Imperfectly experience the moment. Release the need to "fix" it. Surrender to what is before you, and learn.

And we'll continue, deeper into the quest that is all of You.

This Matters So Much: Matt Lavars' Story

We men are often told to soldier on… toughen up… get on with it…

My entire life all I knew how to do was to push my emotions away.

When I was growing up my little brother tried to take his life… Both my uncles passed away from cancer… A close friend committed suicide… yet the only thing I could feel through it all was numbness.

My world was black and white. It was low-level anxiety and a quiet hum of sadness, frustration, and depression.

Then I discovered Ultimate You.

So many other books and educational programs would explain the problem, but they didn't explain *how* I could move forward…

The Ultimate You Quest program gave me the pathway to do so.

Re-educating myself on my emotions through Ultimate You and the Ultimate You Quest program has been one of the most important journeys I've ever been on. Sometimes I've felt uncomfortable. Sometimes I've felt incredibly challenged. But the more I connected with my emotions the more I knew that I was fully capable of feeling every single one of them.

My life went from being black and white to being a beautiful full-color spectrum.

Feeling used to scare me. And now I *love* it!

I feel compassion, love, calmness, anger, sadness, and joy… And I don't feel ashamed to feel them.

Since starting this journey, I have deeper relationships with so many people in my life and I cherish them in a way I never even knew was possible. I've reconnected with my creativity (something I'd always shut down) and have started singing lessons, dancing, home deco projects, basketball, skating, and more... All the things I always thought about doing but never actually *did*.

Life has become so much more fulfilling because I'm more open, more caring, more certain of myself, and now able to discern what's okay and not okay in my world. Coming from a full-time people-pleaser, this is huge for me!

I feel more confident and powerful than I have ever felt.

As a professional speaker and trainer, this shift has completely taken my career to the next level. After sharing my growth and my journey on stage, people would often come up to me and share how much they appreciated my authenticity, and how it helped inspire them to be more open, more vulnerable, more emotional... who would have thought!

I know none of it would have been possible without Ultimate You.

It has transformed my life.

And as you're here, reading this book, go you! I'm so, so thrilled for you. You are so worth this journey. You matter, maybe more than you know. The most important thing you have to do while you are here on this earth is to claim you!

Ultimate You shows you how.

Key Messages

- Emotional intimacy is all about how you turn the key in the doorway of your True Self. You experience your emotions to completion; you're spontaneous without being self-conscious; you are present and listen deeply to others; you can be fully vulnerable and feel empowered; you can empathize while still maintaining your personal boundaries; you never feel a victim to your emotions; and you know when you're repeating a pattern that's part of your conditioning.

- As a child, if you were denied an emotion, you were denied being accepted for being yourself. If expressing emotion was shamed, through being mocked, judged, rejected, or ignored, you internalized this to mean that *you* were the problem.

- There are no "negative" emotions. All emotions are within you and need to be expressed.

- Vulnerability requires honesty with yourself.

- To be your truest you, you must take full responsibility for your emotions.

- There are many ways to avoid feeling your emotions, including defensive and aggressive strategies.

- When moving toward emotional intimacy, start with the seven core emotions: fear, anger, happiness, disgust, surprise, sadness, and anticipation. Know that shame may be linked to any or many of them, and that this is normal.

- Emotional intimacy takes practice: be present to the emotion and simply feel what you feel.

- Learn the language of emotion to increase your awareness of, and connection to, your emotional landscape.

- Know that you and your emotions are as significant as anyone else's.

RESOURCES FOR YOUR JOURNEY

A companion worksheet, an exercise for you to do that relates to this section, a video from me, and more resources are available for you at:

www.ultimateyouquest.com/quest-support

PART III

"I Become…"

We've journeyed to personal responsibility, to our own choices to live consciously, and to how we can begin the unravelling of our own enmeshment. And we've explored and discovered together how our boundaries are vital to our self-esteem, how we can meet our own needs, and how our willingness to be emotionally intimate is a reclaiming of ourselves.

That Self-Esteem Triad is such a wonderfully rich territory of transformation.

And now we're journeying to Part III – to the very heart of the truth of you.

Your Centered Self is ready to step forward into the light. In this, you're going to recognize the lies you've been taught to layer over yourself and you're going to invite yourself to shed those layers and live in the truth of what matters the most to you.

CHAPTER 7

Your Seventh Gift: Your Centered Self

"Maturity includes the recognition that no one is going to see anything in us that we don't see in ourselves.
Stop waiting for a producer.
Produce yourself."

Marianne Williamson

Your seventh gift is the truth of who you are. The truest you. This gift is a challenge for some to accept because it symbolizes you claiming your very core. Everything until now has been in preparation for this gift to be claimed and lived by you.

We've just journeyed through your gift of loving yourself through the restoration of your boundaries; your mindful engagement in your life by becoming the adult you needed when you were a child; and your emotional intimacy. These gifts form your Self-Esteem Triad.

If you *neglect* your self-esteem – your boundaries, your needs, your emotionality – you will meet your Guardian. We touched upon your Guardian earlier in this book. It is the mask you wear to feel safe, protected, and hidden. It's what stops your spontaneity and encourages your self-consciousness. It's on guard against perceived threats such as judgment, rejection, being excluded, and being "found out".

If you *nurture* your self-esteem, you will meet your Centered Self.

The "mask" you wear to protect yourself from hurt is removed and no longer needed once your self-esteem is solidly in place.

" …in relationships as well, we're brought together for real work. Real work can only occur in the presence of rigorous honesty. We all long for that, but we are afraid of honestly communicating with another person because we think they'll leave us if they see who we really are."

Marianne Williamson, *A Return to Love*

Your Guardian wants to protect you from being hurt. It still acts as if you're a child, when guarding you against hurt was vital.

But now you're an adult. So perhaps it's time to ask your Guardian to step aside for a little while and let the You it's been protecting step forward.

What Does Being Your Centered Self Mean?

Being your *Centered Self* is you living as your authentic self without feeling the need to "act" like someone you're not. It's the You that you are meant to be, without pretense, self-consciousness, or shame. She is who you really are. When you are in touch with your Centered Self:

- The one truth – that *you are responsible for your own healing and your own life* – becomes an obvious and lived truth for you.
- *You grow and develop* without apology or justification, both by how you interact with the world around you and within you. Your internal world is as precious to you as any treasure, and you are free of your Tribal Cycle.
- *You speak to yourself with compassion, composure, and kindness.* There's no need to carry around and keep replaying self-defeating scripts, as you know you are your own best friend.
- *You face your problems with honesty,* and you see how, in neglecting your Inner World, you've allowed these challenges to surface. You focus on healing yourself to resolve the external mess, free of drama and manipulation.
- *Your boundaries and the boundaries of those around you are respected.*
- Meeting your needs doesn't involve a crisis, and *you have a healthy expectation that those around you will respect your needs, as you respect theirs.*
- *You have emotional intimacy* with yourself and the core people in your life.
- *You live authentically as yourself,* without self-consciousness or shame, and live to fulfill your own wonderful promise, not to fulfill the hopes of your tribe.

Your Centered Self is the grounded, loving, emotionally connected individual who knows you're enough, that you're worth it, and that you're lovable. She's the You that you are born to be, with the self-esteem to handle what life has to offer, both the wonderful and the worrisome.

Your Centered Self is free of the fragile need to wear a mask to hide her True Self.

Layers of Lies

Back Then, I was a good girl who wanted to please. The me that may have wanted to be rebellious, or feel vulnerable, or be irresponsible was buttoned down, locked up, and invisible. I didn't even know she was there.

And the greatest wound you can experience is
the denial of your Centered Self

When your Centered Self was hurt, overwhelmed, or undernourished, she went into retreat. Your truest You hid, and you were left with the feeling of not being enough. Of not being worthy. Of not being lovable for who you were.

This self-doubt, confusion, and fear took up residence within you. This is the layer you draped over your beautiful Centered Self – and along with her went your natural warmth, spontaneity, love, wonder, creativity, and your ability to feel vulnerable without shame or self-consciousness.

I call this layers of lies our "Uglies". It's the bits we don't want anyone to see, or we feel we need to apologize for, or laugh off, or pretend aren't there.

Into this batch of Uglies, you put everything damaging that you were ever told about yourself, or anything damaging that you sensed about yourself based on how you felt others saw you. You piled into it everything that you modeled by watching your Big People. You piled into it everything you believed was true about your flawed, shameful self.

If you want to meet this layer, listen to your self-talk – the harsh critic within who wants to point out your mistakes, your limits, and your fears.

It goes without saying, doesn't it, that you and I couldn't possibly go into the world with our Uglies on display? No one does. That would be the ultimate shame.

So you learned to cover them up. To bury them. To disguise them. To hide them. To put a mask on to face the world and to appear "presentable". This layer is your Guardian.

It's the surface bit of all of us that we think the world will accept. This public persona sometimes leaks into our personal lives and becomes the decision-maker for us.

When your Guardian was established, the real self – your Centered Self – withdrew from your consciousness and your Guardian self-placed itself in charge of you.

Over time, if you don't reconnect with your Centered Self, your Guardian – this mask – becomes who you think you are.

You forget it's an adaptation. An act. A script.

You Had a Full-Time Job You Didn't Know You Had!

Ideally, you and all the members of your tribe were free to express themselves as themselves and with this came easy acceptance and respect for your emotions.

Mistakes were part of learning – not something to be mocked or criticized. Perfection was not sought as a worthy prize. Warmth. Acceptance. Validation. Differentiation balanced with belonging. They were prized.

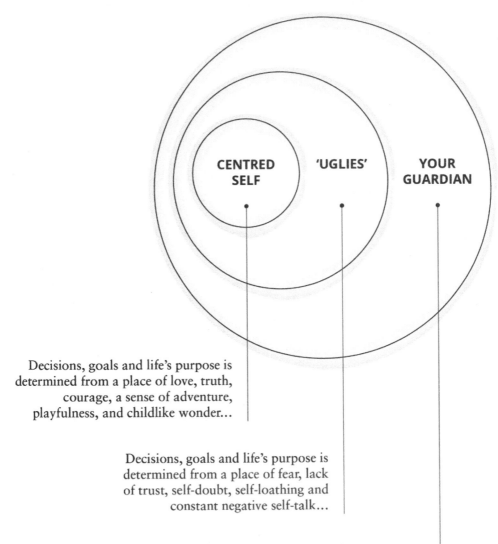

CENTRED SELF   'UGLIES'   YOUR GUARDIAN

Decisions, goals and life's purpose is determined from a place of love, truth, courage, a sense of adventure, playfulness, and childlike wonder...

Decisions, goals and life's purpose is determined from a place of fear, lack of trust, self-doubt, self-loathing and constant negative self-talk...

Decisions, goals and life's purpose is determined from a place of false bravado, in an attempt to build a 'life that gets approval from others'...

And you could be vulnerable. Unsure. Proud. Opinionated. Playful. Serious. Sad. Curious. Loving. Differentiated from the tribe and still be accepted and loved and respected.

This was my experience much of the time, and then sometimes it wasn't my experience. It seems as I reflect back, that I was encouraged through explicit direction... *Don't cry... Make us proud... If you're going to take that tone, then get to your room...* I was also "guided" by overt suggestion... *The expectation that I would be helpful... The vague feeling that I had to be successful... to be a certain way, and not be other ways.*

The Centered Self – me being me – was not wholly welcome. I felt shame if I let my Big People down. I felt a nagging sense of responsibility to be the "good girl". I felt tremendous guilt if I did anything "bad". My Uglies were formed of guilt, wariness, lack of self-trust, difficulty feeling close to anyone, and shame.

And my Uglies were who I came to know myself to be. I'd forgotten my Centered Self and came to see my so-called deficiencies as my True Self. With this, there inevitably came self-doubt, insecurity, self-consciousness, and a big dollop of hating to be wrong.

I couldn't possibly show my Centered Self to the world. No one could see this (warts and all!). I would have been mortified. So I shut down my vulnerability and locked it away.

And my Guardian stepped in and took over. She was the hero. She got straight A's. She was capable. Responsible. Needy but never showing it. Never vulnerable. Always there for others. Problem-solving. Righteous. Domineering. In charge. Showed no weaknesses. A complete trooper.

I became the "level head" and the "sensible one". So the price I paid for my Guardian taking over was to suppress and forget I could feel sad, angry, or hurt. And I also sacrificed the beliefs that my feelings could ever be paramount.

The Guardian protected my Uglies, so they never got revealed. She kept my secrets. Which meant she also hid my Centered Self. This seemed to be what my tribe needed of me for it to keep itself going the way it was, and unchallenged.

Your own Guardian would have come into being through a process similar to this one, but unique to you and to your own childhood experiences. Just know that if your Guardian is still running your show, it takes its job very seriously and has no intention of quitting. It believes it has three primary responsibilities, as follows.

To:

1. Keep your "Uglies" protected and hidden from view.
2. Maintain the tribal status quo.
3. Only allow you to access emotions that are "approved of".

Your Big People didn't know that when their own relationships with each other were filled with insecurity, and unachieved dreams, and broken promises, this created a vacuum that you, the child, rushed to fill. And you filled it to maintain the system. You filled it, not for yourself, but so that the tribal system could keep going, relentlessly on and on, with all its flaws intact, before eventually being handed down to ensuing generations.

Your Inner World Paid the Price

If you recognize this Guardian in you then you know the energy it takes to keep this show on the road. You are cautious in situations where what was hidden may come into view. You avoid experiences where you may feel an emotion arise from the "banned list". You keep the peace while ignoring your own desperate need for reassurance. Or you rock the boat while neglecting your own inner turmoil at feeling rejected.

All of this energy is placed Out There, into the world around you and the people around you. It goes into monitoring the externals to ensure the feedback you are getting about them aligns with what you're accustomed to receiving. If you're accustomed to being treated like the "black sheep" of the family, then your Guardian will show up to ensure that you get validation of that.

If you're uncomfortable with vulnerability, then your Guardian will orchestrate things so that in conversations where vulnerability is present, you will manipulate the conversation to get away from the subject that makes you feel exposed.

Any energy that you expend on going within goes into checking that the Guardian has got your mask firmly in place and no chinks are showing in your armor. Or your internally directed energy may fleetingly feel the disarray of something being wrong, but you're not quite sure what.

Guess what? That fleeting feeling needs your attention.

It's letting you know that as you rely on your Guardian, it stays focused on keeping you safe, not on helping you live Your Awesome Life.

And here's the crucial piece of this puzzle… **the more attention, energy, and focus you place Out There – so you know how to play your role – the less attention, energy, and focus you're placing on your Inner World**. The more you get your Guardian to run the show – as it has since you were a child – the less interior focus you're able to maintain.

You may not even know where to look inside, you're so accustomed to staring out around you, fearful of being unmasked, of being shamed.

The cycle perpetuates itself because in not knowing where to look inside for the answers, you keep looking outside to know you're "safe". You haven't fully developed your Inner World yet, so you can't trust yourself. Thus you avoid new things, stay trapped within your narrow space, and perhaps, stop questioning the way it is.

Because you don't know how to trust yourself, you think you have to rigidly keep playing the role. You may think this is "reality".

It's not.

Let's look at the role of the Guardian a little more closely now.

Meet Your Guardian

Your Big People didn't know that when they felt insecure, deprived, or out of control – anxious – they projected this onto their children. That would be you.

Perhaps your Guardian is the Hero, as my Guardian was. This is the so-called "perfect child". If this was you, you were raised (quite possibly unintentionally) with conditional love. When your parents didn't meet your needs, you interpreted this to mean that you weren't worth the trouble. You learned that if you did well and succeeded, you seemed to get attention and praise. You associated doing well with love. You became a human "doing" not a human "being".

On the outside, you looked capable, conservative, trustworthy, superior, busy, and perhaps angelic. You also appeared to be serious, talented and focused. And you may have had, and still have, a perfectionist streak in you.

You made your family look good, and dysfunctional families like to look good.

The message being communicated was, "How can there be anything wrong in this family if we have a child like this?"

Yet despite what you appeared to be on the outside, on the inside you felt anxious, inadequate, angry, sad, terrified of failure, lonely, ashamed, or numb. Making mistakes wasn't allowed. You couldn't risk being "needy". You had to look like you had it all together. No blemishes. No flaws. Even when you needed support, you didn't know how to ask for it.

And it may have gone further. If you did ask for help, the people around you were (and still are?) so used to you having it all together that you felt ashamed. They made it worse by acting surprised that you need help. Or by being overwhelmed by the request. Or by acting like you were asking too much. It seems you attracted people into your life who could accept your help… and you were masterful at giving it… but who didn't know how to support *you*.

If your Guardian wasn't your Hero, perhaps your Guardian took on the persona of the "Scapegoat". All children have problems. All children get into trouble. Mistakes are inevitable. To be flawed is to be human. In a consciously living family, this is accepted, expected, embraced, and you would have been loved no matter what.

If this describes your tribe, all members are free to be successful, each in their own way; each on their own terms. There is no competition; no race to win. And each of you is allowed to outshine your parents without them feeling or acting threatened.

In the family with a low tolerance for differentiation, on the other hand, this is not the case. If this was you, you were seen as the "problem child". In reality, you helped take the focus off your family's problems by putting the negative attention on yourself.

More significantly, whatever problems you experienced indicated the same precise problems that your family *didn't* deal with. You are the "canary in the coal mine" of what was wrong in your tribe.

You would have looked sullen, strong, rebellious, wild, defiant, rude, tough, and perhaps mouthy. You may have had an unplanned pregnancy. You may have had trouble with the police. You would have likely used drugs. You skipped school.

You heard comments like, "It would be okay around here if you just stayed out of trouble." You may have been mocked with comments like, "That's so typical of you…"

On the inside, you felt, and may still feel, hurt, afraid, betrayed, afraid to trust, rejected and abandoned, misunderstood, blamed, and hopeless.

This feeling of shame often contained within it inferiority and/or the need to blame others, and you tended to remain confused, incapable, or indifferent.

If your Guardian is neither the Hero nor the Scapegoat, perhaps it's the "Lost Child".

It's supposed to be that each family member feels connected to each other. Each member is encouraged to take chances, and your Big People demonstrated risk-taking and problem-solving with grace and ease.

You, in this functional family, received positive attention just for being yourself. You didn't have to "prove" yourself, or shine, or be a delinquent to get attention. You didn't have to conform to receive praise. You and your siblings weren't encouraged to be "seen and not heard" but were allowed to be children.

In a "normal" family, the Lost Child is "the quiet one". If this was you, you were "the dreamer," and you spent a lot of time alone. You stayed away from conflict and problems. Your role allowed your Big People to say, "They're a good kid. If they're fine, things can't be too bad in this family."

On the outside you appeared to be quiet, independent, agreeable, artistic, musical, soft-hearted, invisible, lost in a book, and loath to experience any conflict. You tried to be unnoticed during any conflict. You never wanted the anger to be directed at you. You were intimidated by people who seemed strong and "together".

This personality type often contains within it inferiority, distancing tactics, and dreaming rather than living.

On the inside, you may have felt sad, fragile, isolated, powerless, scared, confused, irrelevant, depressed, and maybe even suicidal. And/or you may have felt resentment or awe at a more successful older brother or sister. In this Lost Child role, you are the polar opposite of the Hero role, and you want it that way. Competing for attention is exhausting.

If none of the above roles fits your Guardian persona, perhaps your Guardian was the "Mascot".

It's supposed to be that, when you were growing up, all the feelings you had were valid. They were taken seriously, acknowledged, respected, and you were given space to experience them. Your viewpoints and opinions were listened to, and clarity was sought when anything was unclear.

A discussion was entered into so that all could learn, grow, and contribute. In this discussion would be validation and sometimes a lack of consensus. This "chaos" is okay in the consciously living family. Each member of it is resilient and self-assured enough to withstand the uncertainty of uncertainty.

The darker emotions... sadness, grief, anger, frustration... have the light of day. They are not denied, shamed, ignored, belittled, shut down, banned, or punished.

If you were the Mascot, perhaps you lightened the mood with humor or antics. You were "the cute one".

On the outside, you appeared to be funny, carefree, charming, attention-seeking, dramatic, lovable, needy, manipulative, and immature.

On the inside you felt, and feel, terrified, needy, confused, left out, helpless, dependent, unsure, lonely, and in need of others to validate you.

Maybe your Guardian has the face of the "Caretaker". You would relate to this if you felt the need to support others rather than be supported yourself. If you felt guilty or uncomfortable receiving support or having your needs met this could be the role you play.

You put others first. You live to serve. You prioritize others.

Perhaps you relate to being the "Designated Patient" or know someone who identifies with this role. If this is you, you're the person who is often sick and needs constant attention. You "force" the people around you into the role of caretaker. Breaking free of the role of caretaker in this situation is considered selfish.

Or your Guardian may have been assigned the role of "Surrogate Spouse." This is a sad burden to have carried. For this to occur, your parents had intimacy issues or were just plain miserable with each other. One of the Big People came to you to meet their adult needs and expected you to be confident, a secret-keeper, and a partner in their life. This is so inappropriate. No parent should inflict their adult problems onto their children.

If this was you, you have probably grown up with relationship issues, and I feel for you. How difficult it must have been to be treated as a mini-adult and denied your own needs when a child.

My clients have given their Guardians different names, based on what suits them. I've heard, "Robot," "Good Girl," "Family Black Sheep," "Auto-Robot". "People-Pleaser" is another typical one.

These roles, however anyone labels them, have within them
some beautiful qualities that you can admire, keep, and treasure.
This isn't about trying to get rid of the Guardian entirely.
It's about figuring out what you love about your role,
and how it supports your Centered Self, and then
figuring out what you've been rejecting
to stay in "character".

There are many ways your Guardian may present to the world on your behalf. It's worth reflecting on how your Guardian guards you now, and what you don't do or won't do because of the limits and boundaries its guardianship represents.

You Have the Power to Choose

Back Then, I was completely unaware that my Guardian ran my show. I thought I was fearful. Intolerant. Judgmental. Turns out, I *am* all of those things… but they're not *all* of who I am. I'm also loving and warm, and passionate… aspects of me that my Guardian, in taking its job so damn seriously, didn't allow to filter through. So I lived in fear.

And with intolerance toward myself.

My Centered Self needed me to wake the hell up.

All the time that I lived on automatic and let my Guardian drive my choices and behaviors, I moved further away from my Centered Self. As a result, My Awesome Life was an impossible pipe dream. My Guardian wanted me to stay at home. Play it safe. Pull the curtains.

Your Guardian whispers to you that it doesn't matter; that one more day won't make a difference; that it's hard; maybe tomorrow… And each moment of denial moves you further away from the beautiful life you secretly imagine for yourself.

This is not about blame. Your Big People experienced the same stuff you did; they felt the same pressures you felt.

This is a systems problem: the system maintains,
as long as you play your role

And as long as you keep your Guardian in charge, you're following your default map, which is your past and all you were conditioned to accept as "just how things are". The numbing, the feeling that you're not quite you, the sense of loneliness… continues.

No matter what was expected of you when you were a child, you now have the power and the freedom… to choose.

And in that choice is the power to *change.*

To keep your Guardian in charge is to live
with the toxicity of rigidity, stuck within the
walls of obedience without context;
it's time to break free

There are aspects of your Guardian that are authentically you. This isn't about changing you. It's about tapping into *other* aspects of yourself that have been neglected, suppressed, and denied for too long.

Your role, when played exclusively, is designed to protect you from hurt and to maintain the family system. It is not designed to provide compassion... compassion risks vulnerability, which risks being shamed... which reminds us that we feel *we* are the problem... which triggers our self-doubt...

Your Guardian is not designed to meet your needs... It has only three purposes: To protect your Centered Self, to maintain the system, and to shut out emotions that aren't "permitted".

It's not designed to fulfill your emotional expression. It can only emote the emotions assigned to it. Anything outside of its range is non-accessible.

Virginia Satir, in her book *Your Many Faces,* shares this: "When I hide some of my faces or have faces that I don't want to accept, then I am in danger of putting on a front. Essentially, I give out bum clues. When I fully acknowledge all of my faces and the fact that I'm in charge of myself, then I can allow myself to feel different ways at different times. I can admit that I am capable of error as well as great success. I can afford to accept myself as a person, and I can more easily grant you the same possibilities. I can deal with real things rather than my fantasy of them."

With your Guardian no longer in charge, you will be free to express yourself in a multiplicity of ways. Your emotional range will grow. Your capacity for intimacy will magnify. Your desire for self-care will expand. Your need for approval will diminish. Your sense of self will come into focus.

You cannot ever really know who you truly are when you wear a mask.

Why This Matters So Damn Much

Your Guardian, to the extent that it runs your life, affects how you feel about yourself and about your life. It impacts the quality of your relationships with yourself and with others. You may tell yourself that it doesn't matter and that you're "fine," but it's shaping your future every moment it's at the helm.

You are due to be your own source of inspiration. Your Awesome Life needs *all* of you. Your choices will move you toward or away from this Awesome Life.

When you learn who is behind the mask, you begin to boldly experience yourself in ways that you haven't connected with since you were very young.

The reunion with yourself is going to be wonderful.

To let your Guardian stop running the whole show
means to let go of one of the most troubling and limiting
aspects of enmeshment: the toxicity of rigidity

To blindly and unconsciously be the only version of yourself that you were "taught" to be is to act as if you're a hammer. To a hammer, everything looks like a nail.

It's to stay locked within the confines of a play you didn't write and don't want to star in (even though you *do* know your lines).

It's to remain trapped within the prison of expectations.

Rigidity is the belief that the way it is now is the way it's always been and is how it must stay. It stifles free expression, shuts down feedback, and locks out differences. It frowns on individualism. It sees compassion and vulnerability as weakness. It seeks to keep the status quo for no other reason than because it harbors a fear of change. And it's definitely against you expressing your differentiation from your tribe.

Your Centered Self is everything rigidity is not. It's adaptability in motion. It sees the moment for what it is, not for how the role must respond to maintain its own status quo. It seeks free expression so that it can learn. It welcomes questions as a powerful source of new perspectives.

Your Centered Self adapts to the moment. To the person. To the needs of the experience.

Your Centered Self seeks to go beyond the tribe for answers.

Your Centered Self isn't interested in how to placate others or secure their permission. It wants to come out of hiding and *be*.

Your Centered Self gives you healthy boundaries, meets your needs, and allows you to access the beautiful tapestry of your emotions without self-consciousness.

To do this, you must give up the rigidity of your Guardian's role. You must defend your Centered Self in a way you could not have done when you were a child. You are going to be for your Centered Self what she needed when you were a child.

Acknowledge Yourself

Hiding your Centered Self within the walls of your Guardian happened because of your need to compensate for experiences in your life that overwhelmed, stressed, or undernourished you. Your Guardian slipped in to run the show when you didn't have the awareness, the power, or the freedom to make your own choices. And the choices you made served you at the time. Doing this kept you safe.

Acknowledge the Guardian, that you,
as a child, adopted, and how it served a purpose.
It has to have served a purpose, or you
would not have taken it on.

Imagine that child. Doing the best you could.

Needing protection. Or taking on the mammoth task of protecting your parents from a flaw they couldn't handle in themselves, or to prevent you from being hurt, or to prevent your parents or a sibling from being hurt. To provide safety for you. Or to provide safety for your family to play out their dysfunction without confronting its causes.

Protect. Prevent. Provide.

You are most likely still running the same show. With the original family system. With your own family. With friends. With colleagues. Your boss.

And with yourself.

The Guardian becomes, over the years, who you think you are.

It's part of you, yes. It's just not *all* of you.

Acknowledge now that you did a wonderful job, as a child, of coping in your family system. You, the child, did what you needed to do.

Now, as an adult… as a Big Person… you get to question the utility of this role. Its reason for existence is no longer necessary within that family system, for you are no longer a child.

Did It Help?

Your Guardian served the purpose of maintaining your tribal system, with its rules, limits, and expectations, so that it could perpetuate itself without challenge. It took over so that you could play your part for your family in keeping the status quo in place, so no one had to look too closely at themselves and face their own anxiety and emotional reactivity. This was important because no one knew what to do with what felt bad. They didn't know how to comfort themselves, or meet their own needs, or express their healthy boundaries.

This is because they had never been shown how to do any of these things. If you'd rejected your assigned role and somehow managed to remain "yourself," your family would not have known what to do with the individuality you expressed; nor with your calm rejection of their rigidity; nor with your open willingness to experience and profer love, care, and respect; nor with your compassion and your vulnerability.

Your Guardian took over, so no one had to deal with the invisible forces that drove their own automatic decisions and actions. It ensured that no one had to reflect on themselves.

You helped, when you had no choice, to keep the Tribal Cycle intact.

The price of the Tribal Cycle is as little self-reflection and differentiation from the tribe's rules as possible

I invite you to question whether your Guardian still helps you, beyond maintaining the status quo.

Does your Guardian help you live the life of your dreams? Because you are headed toward a future that inspires you, or toward more of your past, or will perpetually run from what you no longer want in your life.

Does your Guardian help your tribe fulfill their individual expressions of themselves? Because each member of your family is either living a life filled with meaning or is living in fear.

Perhaps you can see that each person in your tribe has their own Guardian that keeps the whole system moving forward intact and without question. If you see expressions of love, of care, of respect, of compassion, of inclusion, of vulnerability, of celebration, then the people in your family can freely express themselves and without fear of judgment or rejection. If you see expressions of judgment, rejection, shame, fear, hostility, ridicule, anger, manipulation, disrespect, or shame then the people in your family live unconsciously in fear of upsetting the invisible status quo, and they prioritize this instead of allowing each family member to live a life of differentiation and meaning.

The reason why so many people feel a lack of fulfillment as adults is because they've unwittingly left the Guardian of their childhood in charge, and this is only one aspect of them. They don't live their full and authentic selves, so how can they feel fulfilled?

Is this the case for you?

What's Cool?

Your Guardian has aspects that you love and are naturally you. These aspects help feed your internal flame and energize you. These aspects are meaningful and heartfelt parts of you. They suit you…

I was raised to be a Caretaker and Hero. When I believed this was *all* I was, I was empty inside; miserable and confused.

When I realized this projection was just *that*… a projection… and that there was more to me than these narrow definitions, I set out to discover who else I wanted to be.

There are aspects of my Guardian that I love and don't want to give up.

Regarding the Hero aspect of my Guardian's persona, just because I was "trained" to appear as the Hero, it didn't mean there aren't aspects of this that aren't genuinely me.

The Caretaker part of me loves to nurture others, and help them, and coach.

Being a coach is a very natural fit for me. It brings out much of the best in me. I bring this to my friendships, to my family, and to how I nurture myself.

My Hero part of me loves to shine and throw myself into things, and learn, and face challenges. This lends itself to me being a public speaker, and the reason why I've been successful with my businesses. When I face a challenge, this part of me is awesome.

But these are *parts* of me. They are not *all* of me. They do not *define* me. I would not want to be these Guardians, exclusively, all of the time. I've lived it, and it's exhausting. And it wasn't me. Not all of me.

Consider what aspects of your Guardian suit you,
bring out your best, and give you a sense of meaning;
make a decision to keep this wonderful stuff
because it's you and it suits you

I decided to keep all the good stuff. I love that I care about my friends and family and that I can be trusted to be there for them. I love that I bring empathy and kindness to our conversations as well as pragmatism. I love that I am a business person. I love that I can create wealth and help others do the same. I love meeting people, I love learning about people. I love my curiosity, my openness and my sense of adventure.

These are some of the gifts my upbringing has given me.

Perhaps for you, it's that you are a thoughtful, loving friend. Or that you're organized and find it easy to help others get organized. Or that you can be supportive beyond all measure.

Perhaps your Guardian gives you incredible freedom, and you don't feel the need to conform, and you don't really feel the pressure of other people's expectations...

What you love about your Guardian, you keep.

. . . But Challenge Your Own Status Quo

Your Guardian would have shaped, until now, your beliefs about what's possible for you to achieve in the world, your expectations of other people, your perception of the world, which emotions you can tap into and which you can't, your attitude toward love and compassion, and every aspect of how you perceive yourself.

And while there are aspects of the Guardian you've adopted that are wonderful and naturally you, there are other aspects that *aren't* you and lead you to feel incongruent. These aspects are why you feel "different," and cause you to doubt yourself.

For me, it was always putting myself last in relationships and wondering when it would be time to get *my* needs met. It was the constant maintenance of "I'm right and I know." It was the relentless suppression of any flaws, fears, or blemishes. It was my exhausting desire to be on top of *everything*.

It was pretty terrifying to even contemplate not being superwoman. Cue laughter here. But there is real truth to how trapped I'd become within the Guardian's grip.

Perhaps you'd like to consider:

1. What aspects of your Guardian create within you a feeling that you're not being yourself?
2. What aspects of you are blocked, suppressed, denied, or ignored as long as your Guardian is in charge?
3. What aspects of your Guardian are holding you back, suppressing you, or causing you to be someone you suspect you're not?
4. Think about those aspects of your Guardian that you don't love. That annoys you. Frustrate you. Limit you. Leave you feeling empty, or alone.

There will be aspects that don't suit you, and that's okay;
you have the power to choose

The facet of me that was the Caretaker, at its worst, meant that I always put everyone else ahead of me. I never took care of myself. I felt obligated to everyone and was a people-pleaser. My friendships were lopsided affairs where I was always listening, and my friends were always able to rely on me for support. When *I* needed support, they didn't know how to support me, because I chose friends who needed caretaking, not friends who could reciprocate.

As you consider what *isn't* your truth, make a commitment to learn to drop these aspects that keep you trapped within your Guardian self. It's time to invite your Centered Self home!

You will have your own truth when it comes to where you compromise, make excuses, hide your truth, or pretend it doesn't matter. If your Guardian takes the form of the Rebel, this may give you a sense of personal power, but it may cost you because you reject good ideas, given that you won't take advice from anyone.

If you're the Perfectionist, perhaps what you hang onto is your tiresome need to obsess long after it's time to let go.

If you're the Scapegoat, it's your predictable rebellion and your constant craving and need to "prove" how special you are.

If you're the Star, perhaps you have a constant need to prove you're the best, instead of sometimes relaxing and going with the flow.

You may have learned the role of Robot, or Good Girl. You behave. You smile on cue. You're demure when asked if you need anything. You accept being treated like crap by a guy because "Who am I to make waves?"

And the downside to this role?

It stops you from living your life on your terms.

And what about the constant need to "act" happy, instead of actually being happy?

What about the way you sacrifice your feelings all the time?

What about the way you don't ask for what you need? And you've forgotten what it is to be seen and loved and appreciated for who you are, even when you're sad or mad?

Guess what? It's time you messed with these scripts.

Mess With the Script

Who you were told to be, shown you needed to be, encouraged to be, discouraged from being, felt you needed to be... *question it.* You may end up deciding that you like the role your Guardian plays and would change nothing. Great! But at least ask yourself what would happen if you messed with these scripts.

To not examine your life is to not have awareness of the conscious choices available to you or the significance of your internal fire being stoked and fueled by your True Self. And you can't hide from your True Self and make choices to diminish your fire and expect the fire to roar.

It's time to flip the script:

1. Be curious about the aspects of yourself that you've shunned, ignored, or judged until now. If you're the Hero, you've shunned the Scapegoat and the Rebel. If you're the Scapegoat, you've avoided the Hero and the Star.
2. Figure out the roles that your Guardian has made a point of not connecting with, and ask yourself how you'd describe them. Boring? Lame? Too wild? Too emotional? Too cold? Overly pragmatic? Know-it-all? Too good to be true? Self-involved?
3. Consider what parts of you were punished, banned, ignored, or shunned when you were a child. This will give you insight into what aspects of yourself you've been denying yourself since then.
4. Consider that the roles you've rejected up until this point are aspects of *yourself* that you've rejected and denied.
5. Reflect on who your "preferred" parent was. You may not know this consciously. But there would have been one parent who had the most sway over you as a child. Consider what roles they played and what they denied themselves. It will give you insights into what you may have been encouraged or discouraged from expressing.
6. Consider how you responded to this. You may have responded with compliance and become like them. Or you may have chosen to reject them, and thus choose counter-roles in opposition to them.

If you're the Good Girl, then you've rejected parts of yourself that you're going to need to restore your Centered Self. They may include: Wild Child. Rebel. Creative Type. Joker.

If you're the Rebel or the Scapegoat, then you've rejected parts of yourself that you're going to need to restore your Centered Self. They may include: Reliable One. Adult. Professional. Capable One.

And the aspects you've rejected, until now,
are aspects of you. They are part of you. And when you
embrace all of you, you can feel whole and
restore your Centered Self.

So who are you, if you embrace, or at least consider looking at, the flip side roles?

What aspects of these roles are worth "trying on" for yourself?

Because you have been raised in uncertainty, you operate in extremes. You have rejected aspects of yourself that brought you pain or rejection.

They don't have to do that anymore.

Describe in positive terms this wonderful "polar opposite" you're looking at... who is an aspect of your True Self. Describe this aspect in terms of what it would give you, which is currently missing from your life.

Go gently.

Go slowly.

For you're meeting yourself.

This Matters So Much: Jane Cann's Story

I remember the first time I heard about an Inner World, it took me by surprise. I had no idea I had Inner World Needs that needed to be met.

Then when Sharon started sharing about roles... suddenly it was like this veil came down and I was seeing my life clearly for the first time. It was as if Sharon was talking to me directly, as if she wrote this book for me personally.

I remember the moment I finally realized I had the answer to my constant exhaustion and the sense that I was slowly becoming invisible... This moment was when I was listening to Sharon Pearson as she explored how to relinquish our learned roles, to focus on our own need, in order to heal ourselves and to become our Centered Self.

I knew then it was time to resign from the unresourceful parts of my role and reconnect with my emotions, my needs, and my boundaries.

You see, I was living through the lens of a people-pleaser. My life needed approval from others, and my false self was deciding how successful I was going to be in life, in business, in my relationships with others, and with myself.

And creating healthy boundaries as a people-pleaser was no easy task mind you...

Respecting my own needs when my whole life they'd been placed behind others was a challenge...

Reconnecting with my emotions, feeling them, accepting them, loving them...

Wow! That was a journey!

Through Ultimate You, now there's infinite possibilities of who I can choose to be, which has created a wonderful sense of empowerment for me...

I'm deciding who I am, and I love that!

It's giving me the courage to be more open and to experience more of life.

I can be excited and curious and inquisitive and playful and irreverent ... I can stop giving myself such a hard time! I can give myself permission to be vulnerable, to be flawed, to not succeed all the time... and funnily enough, that's helping me create more success.

I'm rediscovering all these parts of me that have been dormant for so long... And I am so grateful for this opportunity, this journey, and for Sharon. It is such a gift.

This is a beautiful, gentle, compassionate journey *back to me*.

It doesn't require any rah-rah. It doesn't need any fanfare.

This is me reclaiming me. And it feels amazing!

Key Messages

- When your Big People wouldn't or couldn't affirm your feelings, thoughts, ideas, perceptions, wants, and needs, you felt the rejection of your Centered Self.
- Being your Centered Self is to live as your authentic self, without feeling the need to "act" like someone you're not. You are free from the need for magical thinking; you grow and develop without apology or justification; you speak to yourself with compassion, composure, and kindness; the problems you have are faced with honesty; your boundaries are healthy; your needs are healthy; you are emotionally intimate; and you live authentically as yourself.
- See yourself as the home of three layers – your Centered Self, which is the truth of you; your 'Uglies', which is the layer created when your Centered Self was not affirmed; your Guardian, which you take to the world as a mask or role so no one sees your 'Uglies'.
- In a healthy family, people have flexible roles. In a dysfunctional family, the roles are rigid.
- The role you took on was a response to your family dynamics. Each of the family members divided up the emotional responsibilites. Your role was created to keep the tribe together, unchanged and unchallenged. The system determined what your role would be; not you.
- Your role may have been Hero, Scapegoat, Mascot, Lost Child, Caretaker, Surrogate Spouse, Robot, People-Pleaser, Daddy's Princess, Designated Patient, or any one of a number of others.
- The aspects of you that you've rejected are indeed aspects of you, and until you embrace all of them, you can't and won't feel whole.

RESOURCES FOR YOUR JOURNEY

A companion worksheet, an exercise for you to do that relates to this section, a video from me, and more resources are available for you at:

www.ultimateyouquest.com/quest-support

CHAPTER 8

Your Eighth Gift: Your Capacity for Truth

"You will become as small as your controlling desire;
as great as your dominant aspiration."

James Allen

You're so close. You've come so far…

You have so many gifts you can draw on and count on in your quest to your own ultimate self.

You're empowered with the knowledge that you're responsible for yourself and your life. You're cultivating the thoughts and habits that lead to an expansion of opportunities to learn and to grow. You live consciously, deliberately focusing on compassionate thoughts and acts of kindness. Your self-esteem is being restored as you constantly maintain your healthy boundaries, your mindful engagement by seeing that your Vital Needs are met, and your emotionality.

And now that you've asked your Guardian to step back and allow all aspects of yourself to step forward, you're getting acquainted with your Centered Self.

At this point, you're ready for a truth you've always known at some level…

You've probably already sensed this… perhaps have had an inkling you couldn't identify.

And yes, it's true… the final part of this journey is for you to know that you are worthy, you are enough, and you are lovable…

Your eighth gift is your capacity for the truth.

"We cannot solve our problems with the same thinking we used when we created them."

Albert Einstein, *Unknown Source*

What is Your Capacity for Truth?

Your *capacity for truth* is one of your greatest gifts. It cuts through the noise and the distractions and distills all the threads of your life into three basic questions:

- Am I lovable?
- Am I enough?
- Am I worthy?

To get to these truths, which are already present within you and simply require you to notice them, is to look to the problems you're trying to solve in your life right now.

To be capable of the truth is to no longer hide behind the distractions, the lies, or the drama that you, and all of us, cover ourselves in.

Remember the garden with a plant in the middle of it that's struggling to flower? The garden is choked with weeds, undernourished and under-watered, and deprived of sun. Would you growl at the flower because it's not growing well? Would you blame the garden someone else has? Or would you weed, water, and fertilize the garden, and clear the branches of the nearby tree to allow some sun onto it?

Most people growl at themselves when they're not getting the results they want in life. Or they blame someone else.

And when that doesn't work, they give up and think they're stuck with their problem. They believe *that's just the way it is*.

> *Let your focus drift from the Safe Problem*
> *– it is simply the flower – and settle instead on what gifts of*
> *learning this challenge presents*

Self-trust comes from knowing you can handle it – whatever "it" is. But if the problem you think you're solving is how to make the flower beautiful without tending to the garden, you're going to keep feeling like a failure. You will keep doubting yourself. *What's wrong with me?... Why does this keep happening to me?... I just don't seem to learn... I'm such a screw-up... No wonder I'm all alone... No wonder I don't ever get anywhere...*

Your truest You knows that your core is comprised of self-love, self-respect, and self-care. You know you can handle "it," and you welcome the journey – this quest – to your Centered Self.

- *You know that when something is out of balance "Out There" it's feedback for you to go within.* The answer is within you.
- *You know that external "wins" don't equate to internal self-love,* and that self-love is earned through restoring your own Centered Self.
- *You're willing to take the journey needed to restore your Centered Self,* including letting go of addictions to external drama.
- *You ask yourself the Three Magic Questions often.*

I trust, after reading this, you will never see your "problems" in the same way again…

Safe and Risky

You, like everyone, have two types of problems.

You have *Safe Problems, which keep you distracted from what really matters.*

And you have *Risky Truths, which you need to face to restore your Centered Self.*

Safe Problems keep you busy, distracted, and focused "Out There," instead of "In Here".

Safe Problems began in the habits of your childhood. You wanted – you needed – to protect yourself from the hurt of being told that you were not enough. Or you conformed to the required role for the status quo in your tribe to be maintained. Because of this, your Centered Self went into hiding. You hid aspects of you that you felt were judged, or were criticized, or deemed to be not lovable.

To hide who we are, and to project this other self – your Guardian self – out into the world, problems began to present themselves. These are the problems inherent in your version of keeping yourself safe from hurt, rejection, and shame.

Perhaps your version of "safety" was to hide your vulnerability and sensitivity. And now you find yourself distant from everyone in your life, wondering how to bridge the gap that you've created.

Perhaps your version of "safety" was to get praised for being the achiever. And now you can't get off the treadmill of work and don't know your kids anymore.

Perhaps your version of "safety" was to be the rebel and prove to your parents you don't need them or their praise. And now you find yourself in short-term and meaningless relationships, with addictions and excuses about why life just isn't going your way.

Perhaps your version of "safety" was to meet everyone's needs in your family except your own. And now you don't know what you need, or who you are, and because you don't know how to figure it out, you stay hidden in people-pleasing mode with no idea what self-care really means.

Perhaps your version of "safety" was to suppress your sadness and anger because you sensed it would be met with disapproval. And now you find yourself with an eating disorder because you only know "control" or "lack of control" and have no relationship with self-love.

My version of safety, Back Then, was to be the "expert," to be uncompromising, and to be super-reliable-no-matter-what. And that meant I was alone because I only attracted people who needed me to fit that bill.

A Closer Look at Safe Problems

The following are some examples of scenarios relating to Safe Problems you may have… These are problems we all created when aspects of ourselves were suppressed, denied, rejected, or shamed in our childhood.

- If I just didn't drink so much, my life would be so much better.
- I really need to get my shit together. Enough making excuses. Enough watching TV. Then I'll really get on with my life.
- If only I could get a boyfriend, then I'd be happy.
- I am so tired of how everyone treats me. No one respects me. If they respected me, I'd be happy.
- My kids are driving me crazy. If only they would behave, then everything would be all right.
- My wife tells me I don't talk to her enough. What's her problem? My dad never spoke, and my parents stayed married for their whole lives. They were happy enough.
- My parents are still telling me what to do, and I'm a grown woman with my own kids. They should quit bugging me.
- I seriously wonder what's wrong with me. If I could figure that out, then I'd be happy.
- I'm overweight. If I could just lose some weight, I'd be satisfied.

- I'm pretty sure one million dollars will solve all my problems.
- I'm pretty sure being skinny will solve all my problems.
- I'm pretty sure having a new car will answer my prayer.
- I'm pretty sure owning our own home would solve most of our problems.
- I'm pretty sure if my parents got off my back, most of my problems would be solved.

Every one of those "problems" share one commonality. They're the "Safe" Problems. They're the stuff you "have" that you think you need to deal with to make your life better. To make you happy. To make you feel that you're enough. That you're worthy. That you're lovable.

But whatever your Safe Problems are, they exist because you have not yet developed your Centered Self. When you suppress aspects of you, you hide aspects of you, and you exaggerate aspects of yourself that you believe will make you more acceptable. In this, you pretend you're someone you're not.

These surface truths (or "problems", however we want to language this), **are created by you as a way of masking your uncertainty about how you should deal with or resolve the deeper truth attached to each particular issue.**

Nearly every single client I have ever worked with has brought their "Safe" Problem to me to resolve through coaching.

They don't get along with their kids.

They want to be more successful.

They want to stop being shut down.

They want to stop procrastinating.

They want to keep doing what they were conditioned and programmed to do – have their Guardian protect their Centered Self from being exposed – and at the same time, they want to achieve dreams their suppressed self can never achieve.

Your goal is not to keep letting your suppression run your life;
your goal is to get in touch with, restore,
and nurture your Centered Self...
your authentic self

That *is* the Risky Truth.

None of this is solved by thinking: What's wrong with me?

None of this is solved by beating up on yourself, no matter how well you've perfected that.

None of this is solved by learning "about" personal development.

You have to roll up your sleeves and do the work. John Bradshaw, in one of his videos, shares how there are two doors. One is marked "Lecture on Heaven". And one is marked "Heaven". How many people are apt to go to the lecture to learn more theory, rather than feeling worthy enough to just enter the door marked "Heaven"? He was sharing the story in the context of co-dependence, but the parallels are there.

You have to defy what you've been told to suppress, and years of conditioning, and make the decision to do what it takes to free yourself from the chains that you're trapped by, and which are holding you back.

Safe Problems – Distractions That Our Suppression Provides For Us

Here are some examples of Safe Problems that I've observed. You may relate to some of them. Each one is designed to keep you nicely distracted on external things, so you don't deal with the real stuff, which is going on internally.

- Procrastination
- Self-sabotage
- Poor management of your finances
- Poor management of your health
- Chronic disorganization
- Any form of addiction
- Overly reserved and shut off
- Overly open and trusting
- Putting yourself in situations where you're treated like the scapegoat
- Putting yourself in situations where you're treated like the victim
- Putting yourself in situations where you're consistently disrespected
- Putting yourself in situations to be admired
- Being attracted to men who use you and leave you
- Being attracted to someone who is only after your money
- Constant overwhelm
- Constant self-sacrifice for others

- Going from one abusive relationship to another
- Wondering constantly: What's wrong with me?
- Waiting for someone else to change so you can feel better/different
- Playing the "role," and not being yourself
- Feeling others are to blame for your problems
- Obsessing about the past
- Constant worry about what other people think
- Over-analyzing everything
- Perfectionism
- Controlling and manipulating others
- Never seeming to have your "stuff" together
- Being let down by your kids all the time
- Being overweight
- Feeling like others take advantage of you
- Believing you're the exception
- Believing that catastrophe is around the next corner, all the time
- Overthinking things
- Thinking you can only succeed if others behave a certain way
- Accumulating wealth
- Accumulating debt

This list is in no way complete. Think about it. Don't Safe Problems just keep reappearing, again and again?

Safe Problems distract you from what was
unsolvable when you were a child...
How do you be loved, and worthy, and enough,
just for who you were

Aren't your Safe Problems keeping you stuck where you are?

What if, instead of trying to solve your Safe Problems, you recognize that they're an adaptation you put in place to shield you from hurt, or to prevent rejection? What if, instead of obsessing about the Safe Problem, you move closer to your Centered Self? And what if the pathway to this isn't found by focusing on the "Safe" Problem, but is instead found by focusing on what matters so much more – your Truest Self, fully expressed.

Risky Truths – The Pathway to Your Centered Self

Now let's turn our attention to "Risky Truths". They're the gold within any problem you and I might face. They're the truth about why our problems seem set on "repeat" and "shuffle".

Risky Truths are constantly, wonderfully, always with each of us, and are beacons on the pathway to our Centered Self

Risky Truths are just waiting for you to recognize that to deal with them is to stop denying yourself, rejecting yourself, judging yourself, and shaming yourself. Risky Truths are *how* you restore your Centered Self. Risky Truths are risky because there's risk in changing how you've approached your life for so long. They're risky because now instead of repeating the patterns of your past, you must find new paths to walk…

Risky Truths are also "risky" because you have to give up habits that have been ingrained within you since childhood, and because you have to challenge the assumptions, rules, and status of your relationships and the world you've created around this shuttered version of yourself.

This shuttered version of yourself came about because you became addicted to focusing on external factors to "make things right". Camaron J. Thomas, Ph.D., in her book *Beyond Help*, shares it best: "We're convinced something 'Out There' will make everything better. So we go looking for something that will make us okay, complete, and perfect, that will set things right in our world. Life becomes, as a result, a succession of very serious choices in which we must, we *need* to make the right one… as if we've only one chance and there's only one correct choice."

Risky Truths are about taking that Inner World journey that matters more than any other journey you will ever take.

Your Safe Problems will be there as long as you don't deal with the Risky Truths

It's not surprising that you haven't put your Risky Truths under the microscope yet. Few people even know they exist, let alone that they are the whole point of life. Your Safe Problems may be different from the Safe Problems that other people have, but your Risky Truths are universal. They are true for every single person on this planet. And they are the pathway to your Centered Self.

The Three Magic Questions

Before we drill down more on Risky Truths, let's check in on the subject of the Three Magic Questions we touched on a little earlier in this chapter. Each of them expresses itself in any number of ways. These truths are simply delightful, impactful, and significant questions you can ask yourself to begin to see your Safe Problems differently and to gauge your relationship with your Centered Self.

The Three Magic Questions are
magnifiers of the quality of your life and
how you feel about yourself

Ponder the questions below and what they mean to you and consider your answers. Be kind to yourself. And remember, whatever answers you come up with, you are on a journey to restore your Centered Self. To be harsh with yourself because you're not sure if you're lovable would be to yell at the flower for not being perfect when it's forced to grow in depleted soil with only a little bit of water.

1. Am I lovable?
2. Am I enough?
3. Am I worthy?

Being lovable is not the same as being loved or being loving toward someone. Being lovable is to know within yourself that you are lovable simply for being yourself and that whether or not someone loves you, your lovability remains intact.

Being enough is not the ego feeling pumped because you succeeded at something. Instead, it's the quiet knowing within you that you are enough regardless of what others say or do, and regardless of what challenges you face. Being enough is you being able to nurture yourself, free of the need for constant reassurance, drama, and control. It's not having to do something or prove something to be accepted.

Being worthy is not the same thing as feeling a sense of entitlement. Instead, it's the quiet knowing that regardless of your past and what you had to suppress and deny yourself as a child, *all* of you is worthy of expression.

I was in my thirties when I recognized how much these questions frightened me. Answering them was terrifying and to be avoided. I was loved and didn't feel lovable. I felt so fragile and insecure that I attempted little in the way of a life. My self-worth was tied up in being right and trying to make sense of a world that was in my eyes crazy for not adapting itself to my world view.

I avoided answering the Three Magic Questions.

Until I didn't.

And while the awareness of what I had created for myself was painful, it was less awful than contemplating the rest of my life stuck in the same tired old patterns of despair.

Try to answer the Three Magic Questions before we move on to learn about Risky Truths together.

Challenging Your Status Quo

Risky Truths can be considered, pondered, and experienced in many forms, and all have their place. They are posed as questions to yourself in moments when you're seeking clarity… when you rise above the self-hypnotic trance you may be in and choose to live consciously instead.

They are the guides that bring you back to the You-you-are-supposed-to-be. They are the questions in which the truth of your Centered Self is contained. They are the beacons with which to set your course.

Risky Truths are the stars in the night sky that remind you that your higher purpose is within you and craves to be experienced

Hold in your mind a Safe Problem of yours that aggravates, annoys, or frustrates you. It could involve a relationship, your finances, your health, your feelings of self-doubt, an addiction, procrastination, a need to people-please, or a need to control others through anger. It could be *any* Safe Problem.

As you hold that problem in your mind, don't fret about it. Instead, allow yourself to suspend the usual worry, anxiety, and self-doubt you bring to it. Just for this exercise, don't do what you usually do.

Now ponder the Safe Problem through the filter of these three risky questions…

- How does this problem keep me safe? (What does it protect me from? What does it stop me from having to deal with?)
- What part of me do I suppress to keep this Safe Problem?
- What part of me don't I trust to keep this Safe Problem?

Someone I know was perpetually falling in love with any woman who paid him attention. One date, and he was declaring to his friends that he had "found the one". He also seemed to fall for women who were impatient with this level of devotion, and they quickly ended the relationship before it had begun. For years, he was sure this was simply because he wasn't meeting the "right" type of women.

Then he asked himself the three questions above.

How does this problem keep me safe? By attracting and falling for women before any real intimacy was developed, he kept himself safe from feeling vulnerable and exposed emotionally.

What part of me do I suppress to keep this Safe Problem? To keep feeling either in love or brokenhearted, he had to suppress any part of himself that was capable of connecting in a meaningful way. He had to suppress his Centered Self's desire for love, genuine curiosity in someone else, the ability to navigate a mature relationship, and emotional intimacy.

What part of me don't I trust to keep this Safe Problem? To maintain this problem, he had to perpetually not trust himself with being able to handle rejection if someone actually got to know him. By being dumped early for his inappropriate confessions of love, he never had to find out what someone thought of him when they really got close to him.

Ponder your Safe Problem with these questions in mind, and allow yourself to consider that what you thought was "reality" is merely a construct created by your conditioned responses to not feeling safe.

Dancing with Your Centered Self's Truth

Your Centered Self craves to be known. Each moment which passes that you deny her is a moment she stays in hiding, awaiting your summons to be encouraged, nurtured, and brought into the light. You can do this through conscious living... through thinking differently from the way you've been conditioned to believe.

Whatever Safe Problem you have, you've thought about it the way you've thought about it through long practice over time. Perhaps you worry about it, or blame someone else, or wish it was different, or pretend it doesn't matter, or talk about it incessantly, or let it distract you from the rest of your day, or let it sabotage other aspects of your life...

However you've focused on it, know that to obsess about the problem without putting effort into changing your thinking is fruitless.

The problem is not the problem;
the problem is how you think about the problem

It's time, isn't it, to consider approaching this a little differently?

Give yourself permission for a time-out from the usual patterns of thinking. No matter how much you're convinced the problem is as you see it, and that you're being "realistic," give yourself the gift of suspending your conviction and replacing it with just 10 percent doubt… Just, perhaps, there is another way to see it.

This exercise is a gift to yourself to look at "reality" a little differently through the questions you ask yourself. Here are some questions to help you shake up how you "see" your situation. Don't rush this. Maybe just pick a couple of questions and take your time in answering them in the context of the problem you're experiencing.

- How does this problem help me to avoid feeling vulnerable?
- How does this problem help me to avoid facing responsibility?
- How does this problem help me hide from being close to people?
- How does this problem protect me from hurt or rejection?

Someone I know had financial issues her entire life. No matter what Rachel did or what she earned, she never had enough money. To get by, she relied on hand-me-downs from family, second-hand clothes, and credit cards. She considered these questions, and the answers were obvious to her, although very uncomfortable.

Her problem helped her avoid vulnerability because she was so often the "victim". No one, she felt, had it as tough as she did. She didn't feel she had to be "there" for others because her problem was so all-consuming. She was emotionally unavailable to everyone because she couldn't stand the attention being deflected away from her and her problem.

Her problem helped her to avoid taking on responsibility for being a functioning adult. She was so "busy" with her financial mess, she didn't feel she had to apply herself to her career, and acted as if her financial drama was a good enough reason for her to be constantly upset, emotional, and uncommitted to her job.

Her financial mess resulted in Rachel feeling inadequate. "Self-loathing," is how she described it. This was something she had felt, she revealed, since a very young age, when her parents had mocked her attempts to be independent. Hiding from people and not letting people get too close to her was clearly the way she had to be. If anyone was too close, they'd know how messed up she was, wouldn't they? And she couldn't risk that.

Rachel isn't reliable, can't be counted on by others, is consumed by her financial problem, keeps people at arm's length, and lets her financial mess come between her and her colleagues at work. All of this allows her to stay safe from being vulnerable, from genuine intimacy, and from relationships based on reciprocity of love, care, and respect. She protects herself from rejection by doing the rejecting first. She protects herself from being hurt by holding the people in her life hostage to her drama.

This is not about a lack of finances, and her problem isn't fixed by having more money.

Rachel got where she is today because of the way she's dealt with and thought about her "problem". More money, with the same thinking, will lead each of us right back to the middle of the problem.

Or, if your job is your problem and you can't find a good one, it's not really about a lack of decent job opportunities. No one's problems are fixed by a great job. If your thinking led you to where you are in your career, and you're miserable, a new job opportunity will not seem great to you, or you will blow it, until your thinking changes.

It's not that there are no great men Out There either.

Your problem isn't fixed when you meet a great man. If your thinking led you to meet a series of ordinary, uncaring men, then a great man isn't going to be attracted to you. You attract who you're ready for in your life, and your thinking created these circumstances, not the men.

Take a few moments – or days – to consider your problem within the context of these questions and how they apply to you. Give yourself the gift of recognizing how the Safe Problem allows you to perpetuate conditioning from your past.

What Would Love Do Right Now?

It takes genuine effort on your part to challenge yourself with the truths we're exploring. If you're doing this, I acknowledge you. It's so much easier to stay on the same railroad tracks and not mess up the landscape.

Each time I've stumbled I've reminded myself that I'm
here to know me as fully as I possibly can,
and I can only do that if I'm
as honest as I can be

One of my favorite questions, when I face a challenge, is: "What would love do right now?" I remember a few years ago our team and I at The Coaching Institute faced what seemed at the time to be impossible obstacles. I didn't know how we'd come through the challenges, but I did know that however things unfolded, I'd have to live with how I conducted myself during this time.

Each morning our team would meet. We had some tough problems to deal with, some tough conversations to have, and some setbacks to be faced. Every day, for eighteen months, was rough sledding. And every day, at that meeting, we would recite… *calm love.*

Throughout the day, when a particularly challenging experience would occur, we would deal with it, feel the hurt or the rejection, and then rally around and repeat… *calm love.*

> *Calm love in the face of adversity;*
> *calm love in the face of judgment;*
> *calm love in the face of hurt and rejection*

Calm love.

Because, no matter what happened, we had to live with ourselves. We would, when we came out the other side, have to face how we'd conducted ourselves, how we'd lived our values – or not, and how we'd supported ourselves and each other when it mattered the most.

The problem… the tough eighteen months… was not the problem. The problem was how we thought about it. And we chose to think about it with love.

What would love do right now?

As you hold your Safe Problem in your mind, set aside your worries about the problem, and see instead the choices you have right now. You can be upset, angry, frustrated, scared, anxious, dramatic… or you can choose to focus instead on bringing your Centered Self to this moment and to the next.

It isn't the problem that is the problem.

Read that again.

And love isn't the whole solution to the problem, but it *is* the solution to how you feel about you, how much you trust you, and how committed you are to restoring your Centered Self.

This problem will pass, but only if you allow it to. And it can only pass if you move through it. If you keep approaching it the way you always have, it will keep reappearing, because how you're approaching it is the reason it's here in the first place!

> *How you're approaching your*
> *Safe Problem is the reason it's here*

There is such a gift in recognizing your role in your life. Life is showing up as a mirror for how *you* are showing up. You cannot remove yourself from the equation. You are the one true constant. Show up with love. Show up to care. Show up with compassion for yourself. Show up like it matters that you're here.

What would love do right now? Love would insist on the best for you. On compassion. On gentleness. On tolerance. On acceptance. On respect. On care. Love would insist on you treating yourself like you matter as much as you do.

Remember Why This Matters

As you raise your awareness – your consciousness – of what your Safe Problems guide you to recognize about yourself, what you have suppressed, denied and rejected about yourself, you can begin to shift your focus from a state of powerlessness to one in which you're empowered.

Your Safe Problems are insights into how you have taught yourself to treat yourself. They are insights into your conditioning. Years before, when you had no say in how you were treated, the foundations for these particular problems were put in place.

You were taught to have these problems, as compared to any others.

You were trained to believe them to be necessary to you. You were taught by what you witnessed, what you were told, what you were discouraged from doing, what you were encouraged to do, what you were punished for, and what you were praised for.

Your Big People taught you that the version of "reality" you experience is actual reality.

But it's not. It's just one version of millions of versions of reality that are available to you.

Just one shift toward more compassion for
yourself, and more respect for yourself,
and the problem itself will
begin to shift shape

Mia seemed to bounce from one awful relationship to another. The men all seemed charming and sincere in the beginning, and then somehow morphed into angry control freaks within a short period. This pattern repeated itself for years, and Mia would bemoan her "bad luck" with men. She couldn't see that she was a magnet for men who wanted to control her. She couldn't recognize that her conditioning – a father who was an alcoholic and a mother who made excuses for it – set her up to only seek out men who reminded her of her father so she could try to get the acceptance from them she hadn't gotten from her dad.

She answered the Three Magic Questions with a solid "no". No, she didn't feel lovable. She felt anything but lovable. No, she didn't feel she was enough, in any way. She felt inadequate. No, she didn't feel worthy of love, of kindness, or of respect.

She answered the questions to guide her to her Centered Self. She recognized that her lack of familiarity with being vulnerable prevented her from valuing vulnerability when she saw it in a man. So she avoided men who would give her the space to be vulnerable. By seeking men who were demanding and controlling, she didn't have to be responsible for her own life. She could instead play the "victim". She could never get close to the men she was attracted to because their Safe Problem was to dominate situations that required love.

The toughest question for her to answer was how this problem protected her from hurt or rejection because it seemed to her she only ever got rejected. After some thought, she realized that by only being with men who were incapable of giving her love, care, and respect, she never had to reveal her True Self and thus risk her Centered Self being rejected. With the controlling men she chose, she was always in hiding. She had never risked being truly known.

By going through this process of self-examination with care and reflection, you begin to build your Inner World and to get in touch with what really matters to you.

When you begin to recognize what matters to you,
you can make new decisions and new commitments
more aligned with this truth

Mia's goal was not to meet a "good man". That was the external construct that would resolve itself when she took care of her Inner World. She committed to building a relationship with herself first. She learned how to trust herself with her vulnerable moments, and how to nurture herself. She learned how to take responsibility for her emotions instead of waiting to see what other people wanted from her. She took time for self-care for her sake, and not so she would look good to men. She distanced herself from relationships she had with people who were incapable of reciprocating love, care, and respect.

Your Turn...

What's a Safe Problem *you've* carried for a while?

Once you've gone through the questions provided, get in touch with the journey that matters...

It could be that you don't know how to be vulnerable and feel safe. Let's take that journey together...

It could be that you don't know how to be emotionally available. Let's take that journey together...

It could be that you feel it's you doing all the giving in your relationships, with nothing left for you. Let's take that journey together...

It could be that you don't know how to have relationships built on reciprocity of love, care, and respect. Let's take that journey together...

Whatever it is, the answers will reveal themselves to you when you commit yourself *to yourself.*

Decide you're worth this. You're worth the journey ahead. You're worthy of feeling loved, and lovable. You're worthy of knowing yourself and loving yourself. You're worthy of feeling care and respect and of giving this as well. You may not know how to create this, just know you're worthy of it and together we'll continue upon the journey...

This Matters So Much: Wendy Marshall's Story

I started this journey at a crossroad…

After forty years, I found myself made redundant and entering retirement. I needed to find a purpose. What was I going to do with the rest of my life?

Ultimate You couldn't have arrived at a better time.

I'd heard a lot of people talk about it, and to be honest, at first I thought it was too good to be true. I thought there must be a catch… it wasn't until later that I realized that was part of the "safe" thinking that had been holding me back for so long.

I was always the cynic, the perfectionist, the "control freak" – I was terrified of making mistakes. Becoming a mother at a young age, it's as though I decided then that life had to be serious… and I forgot it could be any other way.

Since embracing the Risky Truths of this journey, I'm rediscovering *me!*

I've stopped trying to control the "Out There" stuff and instead, I've started to learn how I can trust me…

I've given myself permission to not be right, to make mistakes, to not have all the answers…

I'm bringing back the playful person that's still in there, who's been stomped on by the grown-up Wendy all these years!

As a result, my relationship with myself has completely changed. My relationship with my children and grandchildren has transformed… we're having these beautiful conversations, and they're loving it!

It gives me great hope for the future.

At sixty-one, I finally feel like I've got a life. I feel like I have real purpose, real meaning. I can see my future now instead of living it day by day. This journey has shown me there's more to *me* than I knew…

Everyone needs this!

Key Messages

- Your Truth is that you know when something is out of balance "Out There", this is feedback to you to go within. You understand that external "wins" don't equate to internal self-love; that you're willing to take the journey needed to restore your Centered Self; and you ask yourself the Three Magic Questions often: Am I lovable? Am I enough? Am I worthy?
- Your truth is that you are enough, you are worthy, and you are lovable.
- Whatever version of reality you now experience, move from the "Safe" Problems to the Risky Truths so you can know your Truest Self.
- Safe Problems make up the drama of your life, and they keep you distracted, busy and deflect you away from you believing you're enough, that you're worthy, and that you're lovable. Risky Truths, when addressed, allow you to release your Safe Problems.
- Risky Truths remind you that your higher purpose is within you and craves to be experienced.
- Consider, when pondering a Safe Problem: How does this keep me safe? What part of me do I suppress to keep this problem? What part of me lacks trust to keep this problem?
- The problem is never the problem. The problem is how you think about the problem.
- How you're approaching your Safe Problem is the reason it's here.
- Just one shift toward more compassion for yourself, and more respect for yourself, and the problem itself will begin to shift shape.

RESOURCES FOR YOUR JOURNEY

A companion worksheet, an exercise for you to do that relates to this section, a video from me, and more resources are available for you at:

www.ultimateyouquest.com/quest-support

CHAPTER 9

Your Ninth Gift:
Your Power to Choose

"The self is not something ready-made, but something in continuous formation through choice of action."

John Dewey

One of the greatest gifts you have is your power to choose. If you want your life to be different, then make a different choice. It's that simple. However, too many people continue to make the same choices they've always made, based on their prior conditioning or their lack of differentiation from their tribe. They then wonder why their lives aren't the way they want them to be. Or they've created a desperate whirlpool of survival, scraping by and never looking up long enough to see the rapids ahead.

If you're too caught up in the "busyness" of your day, you will take the most comfortable, most familiar route to get through that day. Even if it keeps leading you to where you don't want to be.

Keep in sharp focus the relationship between your choices right now, and the tomorrow you will experience. Circumstance. Luck. Fate. None of it sways your tomorrow as much as you do.

"When we stand grounded in our personal truth and take charge of our lives, we take the courageous leap of faith that is needed to transcend our fears and walk through the intimidation of others."

Debbie Ford, *The Right Questions*

What Happens When You Learn to Make Centered Choices

When you make *centered choices*, you nurture your Truest Self. You connect with your highest intention and give yourself a foundation of joy in your life. Life has a richness to it when you make choices that are aligned with your Truest Self.

- *You empower yourself when you decide it's up to you.* When you see the connection between your choice and its consequences, you become the creator of your destiny.
- *You get to determine what you create for yourself* with your relationships, your health, your wealth, your chosen career, and your adventures.

- *You avoid the long-term pain of living for the short-term self-gratification* of the easiest choice.
- *You become able to reflect on your life through the focus of your own choices*, rather than wasting energy on blaming others.

Your ability to make decisions is your most powerful resource. Circumstances and your past are not nearly as powerful as this one ability you have and are using every minute of every day.

Your Highest Purpose

So many people struggle to know what their purpose is, and waste years dithering around the sidelines of life, waiting for inspiration to hit them. Your highest intention is not found in waiting, in pondering, in procrastinating, or in wishing it into existence.

Your highest intention is within you right at this moment.

Your highest intention is to restore your Centered Self,
and then do everything within your power to live the
truth of this as fully and expressively as you can

Bring to each day your highest intention through the decisions you make. Know that these choices reach beyond you and touch the lives of those around you. Compassion. Warmth. Love. Inclusion. Acceptance. Spontaneity. All this and more becomes available to you when your Centered Self shows up.

Put Nurturing Your Centered Self
at the Center of Your Decisions

Whatever it is, and regardless of what you chose before this moment, begin to make each of your choices from the perspective of one question:

What choice will nurture my Centered Truest Self?

Allow each decision to be made with your Centered Self in mind. Consider the impact of this decision on your Centered Self. Consider the impact of this decision if it is not aligned with the best interests of your own highest intent.

Choices That Take You Away from Your Centered Self

Your Truest Self is your essence. It's who you are at your core, without the masks and the tribal expectations and the distractions and the Safe Problems. Your Truest Self is your highest expression of who you are.

When you nurture your Centered Self, you expand in self-esteem, self-respect, self-love, and compassion. To do this, you must nurture your truth. Each moment... each decision... counts.

Your intention – your most important intention –
is to nurture your Centered Self, knowing this is your
life force, your energy, and your source of joy

When you make choices that take you away from your truest version of you, you deplete the energy necessary to bring your purpose to the world. Your first focus must be to bring your Truest Self to life. There are choices that will dim your Truest Self and take you away from the path of learning to express that Truest Self as fully and expressively as is possible. This happens by:

- Reacting to what happens around you and to you, instead of being calmly responsive
- Reacting to your day instead of proactively creating your day
- Pretending you're not responsible for your life
- Letting bills slide and become overdue
- Saying you'll do something for someone and then not doing it
- Comparing yourself to others
- Engaging in diminishing or contracting thoughts and activities, like negative self-talk, gossip, letting someone down
- Ignoring or sacrificing your boundaries to "get along"
- Ignoring or sacrificing your needs
- Ignoring or sacrificing your emotionality
- Ignoring someone else's boundaries, needs or emotionality
- Acting as if someone else's emotions are more important than yours
- Not taking care of yourself
- Not living your values
- Living your role instead of your Truest Self
- Not expressing your Truest Self or revealing too much about your Truest Self to someone who cannot be trusted
- Denying someone their Truest Self
- Trusting people for no reason other than you hope that they'll rise to the occasion and then being let down

- Letting anyone try to steal your truth
- Letting anything try to control you
- Trying to get the approval of others
- Constantly seeing the worst in people
- Having a career that leaves you empty
- Marrying or having children because of expectation rather than because it's aligned with the desires of your highest self
- Pretending "this time" doesn't matter
- Not returning texts or calls
- Gossiping about someone, especially if they trust you
- Revealing something confidential about someone you know
- Lying to yourself about what you're going to do
- Placating yourself with distractions, so you don't have to face a difficult task or conversation
- Staying busy instead of proactively progressing with your intention for the day
- Not examining and reflecting on where your choices have led you
- Overeating/drinking/addictive behavior
- Judging yourself or others
- Staying stuck in "Safe" Problems instead of seeking the Risky Truths

I'm sure this list is far from complete, and you'll have your own ideas about how to steal away your truest version of yourself.

If you're on automatic, then you won't see the consequences of these choices. They will just blur into the background of your life without examination. You'll blindly go about your days, weeks, months, and years ignoring your highest intention and disregarding how your choices are driving you further and further away from who you indeed are.

Your conditioning will want to drag you back to the pathway it's most comfortable and familiar with

It will not, for one minute, want you to leave the beaten path of your Tribal Cycle. Even if that path is hurting you, holding you back, making you sad, making you sick, and causing your distress, it is addicted to wanting you to do what you have always done.

If you're anything less than an active participant in the conscious choices of your life, you become prey to your conditioning, and you give in to your lowest instincts and impulses most if not all of the time.

What to Do When You Make Choices That Are Not Aligned With Your Centered Self

Despite best intentions, focus, and commitment, you'll find yourself falling into the old patterns that you want to leave behind. The conditioning has been there probably for decades, and it doesn't want to give up too easily!

You will find yourself drifting away from conscious living and floating into the slipstream of your past. This will subtly creep up on you. It will nibble at your best intentions. It will keep chipping away at you.

The journey to your Centered Self is one that takes place throughout a lifetime. It's not making one decision to change and then it's done. It involves facing the fact that there are layers to yourself that slowly reveal themselves as you ask new choices for yourself that change the trajectory of your life.

The first thing to do is recognize it's happening. It seems so easy, doesn't it? But in the busyness of the day, with constant demands pulling you in so many different directions, you may find yourself drifting into old habits.

Seeing it happen is very important. Step back occasionally during your day and see yourself from a little bit of distance. Consider that your choices in this moment and in this experience are aligned with your Centered Self. Consider whether or not your Centered Self is welcome in the space you're creating.

Once you're aware of this, and you are able to see yourself drifting away from your highest intention, reflect on what your past conditioning is revealing to you.

When you consistently lose the path to your Centered Self or constantly feel the conflict between fear and your highest intention, know that there is an unconscious need within you that is trying to get your attention. Instead of rushing away from the discomfort, sit with it and consider what it's telling you.

Let's say you want to get in shape and you know you need to get moving, eat healthier foods, and cut out the alcohol. You start out strong and then find yourself drifting into some ordinary choices that aren't aligned with what you said you wanted. You keep finding "exceptions" to your new, healthy diet and "reasons" not to exercise.

Reflect on the conditioning that's underneath this. Perhaps you may find that you have a belief that you don't deserve to feel great about yourself, or that you don't believe you can stick to anything that involves putting your best interests first.

Whenever you do something that seems
self-sabotaging or contrary to what you said you wanted,
you will find unresolved conditioning at its root

And it seems the more you want something, or to make a change, the stronger the conditioning will want to remind you of its presence.

Don't ignore the conditioning because all you're doing is putting off dealing with an aspect of yourself that you can heal.

Your mind will try to trick you and try to get you to rationalize choices and behaviors that go against your highest intention. It will convince you to justify the self-sabotage: *It wasn't that important. Who cares? I'll do it next time. I'll do it when the kids have left school. It just wasn't the right time.*

The self-sabotaging, or quitting on a goal, or procrastinating isn't because it didn't matter, or that you're lazy, or that you're incapable. It's that you have unconscious conditioning and it's winning.

And if you don't acknowledge this, and just settle for "I'm lazy," or "There's something wrong with me," or "Who cares?" then you will stay stuck in the pattern of self-sabotage and conflict for perpetuity. You remain trapped in the internal battle, feeling powerless forever.

Suspend all criticism of yourself as you recognize the conditioning that has kept you trapped. Debbie Ford, in her book, *The Right Questions*, shares: "It's important not to criticize ourselves for having these underlying commitments. They arose out of our need to compensate for things in our lives that either overburdened, overwhelmed, or undernourished us. We made these commitments at a time when we didn't have the freedom or the power to make our own outward choices."

Once you've identified the conditioning pattern, give yourself this affirmation:

I needed to hide when I was without choice,
but now I have choice; I am my own Big Person

Let yourself know that what happened was not okay, you didn't deserve it, and it wasn't the best choice for you or your Centered Self. Ideally, say this to a trusted partner or friend and have them acknowledge the truth of this. Validate yourself as much as you need to.

That was not okay. I didn't deserve it;
it wasn't the best choice for me or my Centered Self

For years I struggled with intimate conversations about me. If it was about the other person, I was there for them, attentive, caring, and ready with support. It couldn't ever be about me, because I kept insisting I had no problems, I had it sorted, and it was "all good". I didn't even recognize the conditioning playing out with this. My "Hero" role was in full throttle and in command of my choices and my actions.

Part of me wanted to be seen, to be recognized, to be validated, to be supported, and the part that was in charge of me wanted nothing to do with anything that looked like intimacy or vulnerability.

When I recognized the conflict that was going on within me, I was shocked, because I'd gotten so good at listening to my conditioning that it hadn't even occurred to me that anything was wrong. I was proud of my "strength," not realizing that my fear was really in charge and running the show.

I was terrified of intimacy and vulnerability. My conditioning told me that people would judge me, and I would be rejected, which had been my experience when I was growing up. *You're not going to cry, are you?*

I didn't criticize myself. Instead, I acknowledged my Tribal Cycle at work. I acknowledged myself for identifying a pattern of behavior that was hurting me and preventing me feeling close to people.

I affirmed that this had been conditioned into me before I'd had a choice.

I told my husband about what I'd identified, and he validated me.

He didn't mock me. Shut me down. Tell me he didn't have time to hear this. He didn't shame me. He listened and affirmed that what happened to me wasn't okay, and I didn't deserve it.

This was a revelation to me. So... I could share something that hurt, and the other person wouldn't judge me as being weak? How was this possible? Could it happen again? With another person?

You may be reading this thinking, *What is the big deal?* I appreciate that my journey isn't yours. To me, it was the biggest, most significant deal. It was seismic in terms of its impact on me.

And so began the process of making a new choice – one that propelled me toward my Centered Self, not toward my fears and my past.

Make a new choice, right now, based on who you're becoming, and free yourself from playing the small game of fear

The Answers Are Already Here

When you discover another opportunity to uncover your conditioning, you will begin to lose the fear around it and access joy instead. As you become more comfortable with focusing and nurturing your Centered Self, the conversation you have with yourself becomes easier. It becomes an adventure... *I've found another way to move forward with my life! Awesome!*

> *When you are stuck in a pattern of behavior that seems*
> *contradictory to what you say you want,*
> *this is your conditioning in action*

Once you've identified the conditioning and walked yourself through the above process, begin to ask yourself some questions to help you restore your Centered Self's truest intentions. You need to ensure that you can let the conditioned patterns of behavior go and move toward what is going to serve your highest intention.

Now try and answer the following questions:

- Where are you not taking responsibility for yourself and your choices?
- Where are you focused on contracting thoughts and beliefs, rather than expansive thoughts and beliefs?
- Are you supporting yourself through this process with compassion and kind self-talk?
- Are you clear on your personal boundaries in this experience and are you living them?
- Are you nurturing yourself through a daily practice of mindful engagement? Are you taking care of your needs?
- Are you being emotionally honest with yourself? Are you being emotionally honest with someone else?
- Is your role in charge right now, or your Centered Self?
- Are you focused on the Safe Problem or are you considering the Risky Truths?
- Are you giving yourself the gift of validation for the conditioning that you never chose? Are you gently reminding yourself that this was not okay and that you deserve better?

Questions give you the pathway through your challenging situation. If you keep asking the questions that have held you back, your self-esteem will drop, you'll feel powerless, and you'll become even more entrenched with the battle between your conditioning and your highest intention.

Questions to Avoid as You Make Empowered Choices

There are empowering questions to ask yourself to help you release your conditioning. There are also questions you may have asked yourself in the past that would cement the problem and prevent you from accessing and restoring your Centered Self.

Questions to avoid:

- What's wrong with me?
- Why me?
- Why isn't this working out?
- Why can't they just… ?
- When do I get a break?
- Is this a sign I should quit?

Situations to avoid:

- Anything that blames you
- Anything that blames someone else
- Anything that keeps you looking back to your past with recrimination
- Feeding the emotional reactivity of those around you through "tension tagging"

Questions to Ask as You Make Empowered Choices

Your power to choose exists, whether you believe you're using it or not. Not choosing is a choice. Deferring to someone else, instead of making your own decisions, is a choice. Blaming someone else is a choice. Staying stuck in a situation that doesn't serve you is a choice. Having that second serving of ice cream is a choice. So is going for a walk instead. You choose your words with the people you're with. You choose what to focus on in your day and in your life. You choose whether this moment will be filled with gratitude or with resentment. You choose, even when it feels that you're powerless to do so.

And yes, powerlessness is a choice.

There are questions you can ask that will help you move towards making more empowered choices for yourself. These questions shape your focus and help to guide you toward the highest intention for yourself.

- Is this choice keeping me stuck in my past or will it help me to restore my Centered Self?
- Is this choice about me avoiding responsibility or about me owning my own life?
- Am I focused on my fears with this choice or on where I'm heading?
- Am I seeking instant gratification with this choice or am I focused on my long-term fulfillment and highest intention?
- Am I letting myself get caught in the Tribal Cycle with this choice or am I seeking to learn more about my own unique qualities?
- Is this choice being made by my Guardian or by my Truest Self?
- Am I making the easy-way-out choice or am I choosing the path that will sustain and nurture me?
- Is this a choice based on self-sabotage or a choice based on self-love and self-care?
- What is the most loving choice I can make for myself right now?

These questions are designed to help you release your conditioning and embrace new pathways for yourself and for your compelling future. Their focus is on directing your mind to the ways to restore your Centered Self so that you slowly lose the neuro-pathways to your disempowerment and develop the neuro-pathways that can provide you with fulfillment, gratitude, and self-love.

It takes time, and repetition, and a desire within you to be greater than the conditioning you adopted before you had a choice.

And as you embrace your Truest Self, know that you are in every way lovable, worthy and enough.

This Matters So Much: Zarnia Wilson's Story

I always felt like something was missing in my life, I just didn't know what. I have a beautiful family that I adore and wonderful friends – but there was just something missing. I flitted from job to job throughout my life, getting caught up in the "busyness", and just kept waiting for that something to happen for me…

Discovering Ultimate You was such a revelation.

It came as a shock. Nothing was going to happen for me… I learned that it was *my* choice, *my* decision, *my* action today that was going to shape my tomorrow. I remember hearing Sharon list the kind of choices that were diminishing me and thinking… Wow, that's me, I do that! And that! And that too! I've been doing that for years! No wonder something was missing for me... I, me, my Centered Self... I was missing from my own life!

It may sound simple, but I finally realized... I wasn't going to be rescued. I had to rescue myself! I had to start making Centered choices that were aligned with who I really am...

That began a life-changing journey for me.

With Ultimate You in hand, I began to ask myself better questions, more empowering questions. I learned how to talk to myself differently, how to validate my experiences, and how to do that for others. I started to see the difference between the choices I would have been conditioned to make versus the choices I am now free to make...

And they have been some of the most courageous, most astounding, most rewarding decisions I have ever made. Even though it hasn't been an easy journey... and in fact, the raw vulnerability I've unearthed has made me want to stop, hide, and retreat numerous times... now I know with absolute conviction that every time those fears and emotions come up, I'm healing, I'm worthy, and I'm enough.

The more I'm stepping into my power, the more I'm making life happen *for* me, instead of letting it happen *to* me...

I'm now in a wonderful job that I love, making more of a difference than I ever have. I'm closer to my children than I've ever been (we now have beautiful in-depth conversations about everything!)

And, perhaps most importantly, I'm finally living my life on my terms...

Key Messages

- When you learn about centered choices, you nurture your Truest Self. You empower yourself when you decide the outcome of your life is up to you; you get to determine what you create for yourself; and you avoid the long-term pain of living for the short-term self-gratification of the easiest choice.
- Your highest intention is to restore your Centered Self and then do everything within your power to live the truth of this as fully and expressively as you can.
- When you make choices that take you away from your truest version of you, you deplete your energy, making it difficult to fulfill your purpose in the world.
- Your conditioning will want to drag you back to the pathway you're most comfortable and familiar with. Whenever you do something that seems self-sabotaging or contrary to what you said you wanted, you will find unresolved conditioning at its root.
- Ask yourself questions that empower your choices, such as: Is this choice keeping me stuck in my past or will it help me to restore my Centered Self? Is this choice about me avoiding responsibility or about me owning my own life? Am I focused on my fears with this choice or on where I'm heading?

RESOURCES FOR YOUR JOURNEY

A companion worksheet, an exercise for you to do that relates to this section, a video from me, and more resources are available for you at:

www.ultimateyouquest.com/quest-support

Epilogue:
My Ultimate Gift to You…

This journey – this quest – is by far the most important journey I've ever undertaken. It's challenging. Sometimes lonely. Sometimes confounding. I sometimes feel like I'm getting nowhere, and then feel I've taken a leap of consciousness and arrived at an entirely new place in my heart.

To recognize that your internal journey is as important, or *more* important, than what you do "Out There" is, for some, an unfathomable mindset to adopt. After all, you can see the house you bought, you can see what's in your bank account, you can see your health improve with exercise. The "tangible" so often is bestowed with the label of the "real".

I believe the "real" is the invisible. It's the smoky, out-of-focus, and difficult-to-define inner work. You may not have words for it, but you feel a different truth – one that cannot be denied – within you. I believe the invisible is the real, and the visible is the illusion. The illusion is seductive, enticing, and distracting. It's so much easier to pursue a career than pursue inner consciousness!

So my last gift to you is just this… You're worth the inner journey. You are enough. You are lovable. I don't care what you say in protest, or how much "proof" you have to the contrary, your Centered Self is nodding along with me, because it knows the truth.

It will be challenging. You will feel you've lost your way. You will doubt the progress you make as you slip back into old conditioned habits. But you will have breakthroughs. You will feel disappointment, grief, and overwhelm. But you will also feel joy, freedom, and acceptance. And through it all, your Truest Self is cheering you on, waiting for the invitation to step forth and resume her rightful place in your heart.

Acknowledgments

The Ultimate You Quest movement began several years ago when I recognized that my "Inner World" didn't match the success of my "Out There" World. And I wanted to know why. I also noticed clients and members from The Coaching Institute community struggling with self-doubt, procrastination, perfectionism and other forms of self-sabotage. Given the access to the answers to these problems that were available, why weren't they simply solving them and moving on with their lives?

I also saw a pattern, which matched my own experience, of people not connecting at the deepest level. People were communicating. Coaching. Hanging out together. But they weren't diving deeply into their own truths.

At the same time, I saw an unraveling of, or perhaps it's a magnification of, human behavior on social media. Shaming people. Assuming the worst. Assumptions. Quick judgments. People being condemned for something they did years before that demonstrated no more than poor judgment and youth.

I wanted to figure out what was going on.

For years, the question that had nagged at me was: What is the ideal community for us to live in?

What would be this community's attributes?

What would it look like?

What would we value? Avoid? Encourage?

Of course, I recognize that for every person who is asked this question, five answers can present themselves.

But it's still, I believe, a worthy question. And the answer is important.

Because I don't believe enough of our leaders are thinking about it. And because if we don't focus on it, we're going to get whatever the most dominant voices decide for us.

My answer to the question goes something like this...

The ideal community would:

1. Teach love, compassion, and respect.
2. Teach how to handle ambiguity and complexity and nuance.
3. Encourage its members to learn, including through mistakes, and through handling setbacks.

The ideal community would celebrate diversity… not by the easy-to-recognize-and-label traits of race, religion or sexual orientation, although all of this is welcome, but of ideas.

The ideal community is filled with members who assume the best intentions of others and seeks to find the good faith of others, even when it seems to be missing.

The ideal community would allow someone to make a mistake, to apologize, and then would assume that everyone around them could contribute to their healing through teaching, not through shaming or shunning.

The ideal community would practice discussion without characterizing the "other" side as "bad," or by labeling them through their ideology, but through seeking to understand with genuine curiosity.

The ideal community would encourage openness, curiosity, adaptability, new ideas, exploration while keeping what works and the traditions that provide comfort.

The ideal community sticks by its members, not when they are winning, but when they are down and out, have fumbled, have lost, or have been shamed.

In this community, there is no mob-mentality or demands for people to get "what they deserve" when they make a mistake. There is justice, not vengeance. There is a big difference.

I like the sound of this community very much. So much so that I began to reflect, study and seek ideas as to how such a place could come about.

We have, through The Global Success Institute, online groups and training on our campus where we get to hang out together, study, compare ideas, share thoughts, support one another, challenge one another, and learn how to be a part of something bigger than ourselves in a meaningful way.

It became the first foray into creating the community I believed would be the most inclusive, the least exclusive, and the most inspiring.

So far, it's working. We have our breakdowns, on occasion. Someone is invited in who has no intention of seeing the good faith intentions of others, or who behaves in such a way that "good faith" would be a generous and foolhardy gift to extend to them.

But for the majority of us who hang out there, it's as I described. It takes work. Monitoring. Feedback. Reminders of our standards. Discussion about what's reasonable and what's a violation of someone's boundaries.

And I'm aware that these groups are microcosms where we, the team at The Global Success Institute, get to decide what happens.

But I became hopeful by what I saw. People free from the fear of judgment behave more freely. They become more generous of their time, efforts and kindness. They share ideas. They risk a little more in the pursuit of their dreams. They let go of old conditioning and try on new thoughts.

They shine.

They start to believe in themselves.

They reignite their dreams.

So then the question becomes: Who do we need to be to create the space for such communities to become more widespread?

And that's where Ultimate You came about.

Who we need to be is everything in this book. We can create communities where we can thrive when we take care of ourselves, embrace uncertainty with the knowledge we can probably handle whatever comes along, and dare to figure out who we are when we're not fulfilling our unspoken promises to our tribe.

This quest is explored because of, with, and through, so many people.

My family, so precious, all doing the best we can. I am who I am today because of you, and anything I do or achieve is because of us. My mum is the loudest and most enthusiastic cheer-squad a writer/coach/business person learning to live could ever wish for.

My husband, "JP," my biggest fan, seeing in me only the good, always believing, even when I get lost, and always loving. Thanks for making the year of this book so wonderful.

John Assaraf, one of the kindest people I know, thank you for your constant and unwavering encouragement. You're one of the good ones.

Jennifer Slack, thank you for showing me, way before I realized I was ready, who I am under my layers of stuff.

Tina Vercillo, you champion me through all of it with compassion and your steady presence. Hey, Caira, you rock.

Joe Pane, steady gaze on your True North, and a friend who sees my best. You teach me what it means to be loyal and brainstorm the geeky details with me.

Elysium "Glam" Nguyen, constant warrior for our cause, passionate advocate for our standards, unflinching seeker of excellence. I couldn't ask for a better wingman or stronger defender of what we do.

Matt Lavars, always stepping forward to learn, grow, and serve. You always have my back, and I love seeing how you bring your own quest for your Truest Self to life.

Ilsé Strauss, when so many people scattered, you stayed the course. Your humor and kindness are awesome, Amazon Woman. Your friendship and support are tireless and so appreciated.

Letitia "Teash" Owen. So many nights fighting the good fight, not one backward step. You see the gaps, fight for the standards and always remember why we do what we do.

Thank you, Mike Jones, Angela Martens, Trang Ho, Michelle Stewart and The Global Success Institute team.

Thank you to Ultimate You Inner Circle members, Adrian Butcher, Alan Williams, Alison Swinbank, Alyson Williams, Amanda Harris, Amy Taylor, An Sneyers, Andrew McLaren, Anne Shaw, Annie Toscher, Belinda Brown, Bella Wunderlin, Ben Burt-Smit, Bronwyn Stedall, Caleb Lesa, Carlas Canache, Christiane Anderson, Christine Ross, Claire Markwick, Claire White, Concetta Scarcella, Cori Sanders, Courtney Ellis, D'Anne Cowie, Dawn Canale, Dawn Favaloro, Deborah Kleinert, Deborah Stav, Dee Webb, Denise House, Denise Gill, Dominic Dolan, Dora Kozulin, Dr. Shahid Yamin, Edwina Kable, Ellenor Cox, Eunice Chan Healey, Fiona Damon, Fiona Morgan, Freda Ackroyd, Geraldine Morris, Grace Reynolds, Ha Le Thai, Helen Morse, Herminia Paubsanon, Jacqui Barns, Jane Cann, Jane Willson, Janet Hutton, Jan-Leigh Matchett, Jeanette McPetrie, Jenni Albrecht, Jennie Markovina, Jenny Williams, Joanne Hewlett, Jody Henderson, John Anderson, Jolanta Debek-Kozyra, Jon Giaan, Judith-Rose Max, Judy Potgieter, Juliana Nkrumah, Julianne Mureau, Kat JY Chen, Katherine Robertson, Katrina Peate, Kelly Petering, Kristy Ambrose, Kylie Chapman, Kym Smith, Lauren Johnston, Leah Mayne, Leanne Costantino, Leanne Wakeling, Leigh-Anne Sharland, Lia Zalums, Lily Gubbay, Lynor Baker, Mandi Pour Rafsendjani, Marcelle Burrows, Margaret MacDonald, Margaret Meyer, Mariana Ardelean, Mary Jensen, Mary Palaric, Matthew Adams, Maureen Wise, Melina Skidmore, Melo Kalemkeridis, Michael Edwards, Michael Hawkins, Michael Lai, Michele Ripper, Michelle Cowell, My Nguyen, Naomi Page, Naomie Martelli, Natassia Chua, Nena Borovic, Nerida Wirriganwalters, Nicole Stafford, Nola McDowell, Paulina Chong, Phil Sealy, Phillip Evans, Prudence Marie, Rachel Rabayov, Ramon Herrera, Rashid Siddiqui, Robert Cummins, Robyn Gartrell, Robyn Jordan, Sally Garrahy, Sally Permezel, Samantha Clough, Samantha De Mel, Samantha Zantor, Sandra Starr, Soraya Toone, Stephen Gregory, Sue Arand, Sue McGrath, Sue Stevenson, Susan Mckenzie, Suzanne Duncan,

Teresa Twining, Terry Doukakis, Thea Wiggins, Tien Chong, Tom Kippenberger, Vesna Anackov, and so many others…

Thank you to the many people who step up each day to bring our dream into reality. The facilitators, mentors, and guides who serve each and every day and always bring their openness and willingness to serve. Without you, none of this is happening.

There's the team that helped get this message out there… Bill Gladstone, Anne Dillon, Devon Blaine.

And always, there are the supporters, who believe in what we do, who love and share our vision for a community filled with quiet possibility, who see their own potential and dare to make it a reality. You inspire me every single day.

How do I even begin to thank the thousands of people who are now a part of this, through The Global Success Institute and through the Ultimate You Quest community?

If ever I was to waver in my mission, you are an easy reminder of why this matters. You're amazing.

Connecting With Our Communities

You're here. You're making the time for you. You're starting the quest to your own ultimate you... and that matters so much. It's a journey to be taken with support, with champions, with the community of like-minded people who are here to celebrate you each step of the way...

Here are all the ways you can start connecting with the Ultimate You Quest community today, wherever you are in the world:

Ultimate You Book Club: Join in the global conversation with like-minded people who are journeying through the book...

www.ultimateyouquest.com/book-club

Ultimate You Quest Global Telecast: Deep dive into the Ultimate You message with me and connect with Ultimate You Quest members around the world on this global telecast...

www.ultimateyouquest.com/telecast

The Global Success Institute Gratitude Wall: Acknowledge someone, celebrate you, share a moment of gratitude on The Global Success Institute Gratitude Wall and see what others are grateful for today...

www.globalsuccessinstitute.com/gratitude

The Coaching Institute Community: Discover The Coaching Institute community, join in on live classes, connect at live events, and meet amazing Ultimate You Quest coaches...

www.thecoachinginstitute.com.au/community

Write to the Team: We would love to hear from you... what you're loving on your quest, what you're discovering about you, and how we can support you even more. Write us at...

support@globalsuccessinstitute.com

References

Allen, James. *As a Man Thinketh. Dover Publications Inc.,* New York, 2007

Bach, Richard. *Jonathan Livingston Seagull.* New York: Harper Thorsons, 2014.

Baker, Dr. Dan, and Cameron Stauth. *What Happy People Know.* Rockport, Mass.: Element Books, 2003.

Bradshaw, John. *The Family.* Video.

———. *Healing the Shame that Binds You.* Deerfield Beach, Florida: Health Communications, Inc., 1988.

Brown, Ph.D., Brené, *Daring Greatly.* New York: Penguin Random House, 2012

———. *The Gifts of Imperfection.* Center City, Minn.: Hazelden Publishing, 2010.

Canfield, Jack. *The Success Principles.* Rockport, Mass.: Element Books, 2005.

Dewey, John. *Democracy and Education,* Hollywood: Simon and Brown, 2011.

Dispenza, Dr. Joe. *Breaking the Habit of Being Yourself.* New York: Hay House, 2012.

Dweck, Dr. Carol S. *Mindset: The New Psychology of Success.* New York: Random House, 2017.

Ford, Debbie. *The Right Questions.* New York: HarperCollins, 2003.

Forward, Susan Ph.D., *Toxic Parents,* New York: Bantom, 2002.

Harris, Sam. *Waking Up: A Guide to Spirituality Without Religion.* New York: Simon & Schuster, 2015.

Kelly, Matthew. *The Seven Levels of Intimacy.* New York: Beacon Publishing, 2005.

Klein, Ph.D., Stefan. *The Science of Happiness.* New York: Marlowe & Company, 2006.

Masters, Ph.D., Robert. *Emotional Intimacy.* Boulder, Colo.: Sounds True, Inc., 2013.

Miller, Alice. *The Drama of the Gifted Child.* New York: Basic Books, 1997.

Needleman, Jacob, and John P. Piazza. *The Essential Marcus Aurelius.* New York: Tarcher Cornerstone Editions, 2008.

Parker, Ph.D., Holly. *If We're Together, Why Do I Feel So Alone?* New York: New American Library, 2017.

Rosenberg, Marshall B. *Non-Violent Communication.* CA.: PuddlerDancer Press, 2015.

Satir, Virginia. *Conjoint Family Therapy.* Mountain View, Calif.: Science and Behavior Books, Inc., 1983.

———. *Your Many Faces.* New York: Celestial Arts, 2014.

Thomas, Ph.D., Camaron. *Beyond Help:* Bloomington, Ind.: AuthorHouse, 2011.

Weeks, Mike. *Un-Train Your Brain.* New York: Vermillion, 2016.

Williamson, Marianne. *A Return to Love.* New York: HarperOne, 1996.

Note: Throughout the book you may have noticed sections where I have drawn on my previous book, Ultimate You: Quest Edition. I didn't want to spoil the narrative flow by saying this each time in the text. My personal stories, especially, are in this book, and I believe form an important role to help readers connect with the ideas of Ultimate You.

Index